BirthSkills:

For Mind, Body & Baby

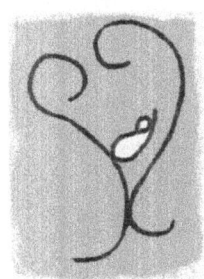

BirthSkills: For Mind, Body & Birth

Author: **Read, S. P.**

All rights reserved. No part of this publication may be reproduced, stored in a retrieval system, or transmitted in any form or by any means, electronic, mechanical, photocopying, recording or otherwise, without the prior written permission of the publisher.

Copyright © 2012 **Shari Read**

Edition: **Second Edition**
ISBN: **978-0-9873579-0-8**

Publisher's Disclaimer

The information, views, opinions and visuals expressed in this publication are solely those of the author(s) and do not reflect those of the publisher. The publisher disclaims any liabilities or responsibilities whatsoever for any damages, libel or liabilities arising directly or indirectly from the contents of this publication.

A copy of this publication can be found at the National Library of Australia.

This work has been inspired by many, the beautiful mums and dads I have had the privilege to work with over the years; my own beautiful children who constantly inspire and motivate me to continue on this path; my brave mother who's resilience I admire greatly; but most of all, my amazing husband who turned me around and set me on this path, he showed me the way and continues to encourage me to keep walking; with all my love.

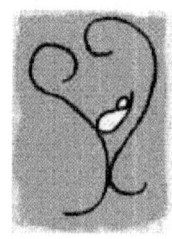

About the author...

Shari has a PhD in social psychology and formal training in clinical psychology, hypnotherapy for childbirth and childbirth education. Shari works as a yoga & meditation teacher and psychotherapist specializing in pregnancy & postnatal wellbeing and women's health.

As well as working with hundreds of pregnant couples over the years, Shari has had two children, both born naturally using the techniques described in this book.

Shari wrote this book with the goal of providing an informative and practical guide to preparing for a calm and confident childbirth experience using mind/body techniques.

TABLE OF CONTENTS

MY JOURNEY 11

INTRODUCTION 17

BIRTH STORIES TO INSIPRE 22

One More Birthing Story… 34

CHAPTER 1 AWARENESS 38

THE FEAR/TENSION/PAIN SYNDROME 45

THE FIGHT OR FLIGHT RESPONSE 48

HOW FEAR AFFECTS LABOUR 52

THE PROCESS – PART 1: HOW THE UTERUS WORKS 55

WORKING WITH YOUR UTERUS DURING LABOUR 62

THE PROCESS – PART 2: HORMONAL ACTIVITY DURING LABOUR 64

WORKING WITH YOUR HORMONES DURING LABOUR 69

#1 Checking In – Self-Awareness Exercise 72

CHAPTER 2 TRUST 73

DEVELOPING TRUST THROUGH FOCUS 74

TRUST AND HYPNOSIS/DEEP RELAXATION 76

USING HYPNOSIS FOR THE MANAGEMENT OF PAIN 83

THE PROCESS OF SELF-HYPNOSIS 87

MANAGING PAIN DURING BIRTHING 91

TERMINOLOGY FOR A CALM, CONFIDENT, WELCOMING BIRTH 98

#2 Checking in – Self-Awareness Exercise. 100

CHAPTER 3 WORK 101

BREATHING TECHNIQUES 102

BASIC PHYSICAL RELAXATION TECHNIQUES 116

Progressive Relaxation Script 118

PRE-NATAL BONDING 124

Loving Welcome Relaxation Script 129

IMAGERY AND VISUALISATION 131

Triumph Meditation – For Fear Release 135

Rainbow Chakra Script 137

MASSAGE 146

AFFIRMATIONS 156

Affirmations *158*

Affirmations for an Awaiting Father *160*

RELAXATION DEEPENING TECHNIQUES 161

Rapid Relaxation Technique (5,4,3,2,1) *161*

Birth Companion's Deepening Script *163*

PREPARING YOUR BODY FOR BIRTHING 166

PELVIC FLOOR MUSCLE EXERCISES 171

PERINEAL MASSAGE 174

DISTRACTION PRACTICE 177

#3 CHECKING IN – SELF-AWARENESS EXERCISE 180

CHAPTER 4 CHOICES 181

BIRTH CHOICES 182

CHOOSING A COMFORTABLE POSITION FOR EFFICIENT LABOUR AND BIRTHING 186

THE USE OF WATER FOR LABOUR AND/OR BIRTH 191

ESTIMATED DUE DATE - EDD 193

SIGNALS THAT REQUIRE YOUR ATTENTION – SPECIAL CIRCUMSTANCES 150

BRAXTON HICKS SURGES 194

INDUCING LABOUR – Medical v. alternative induction methods 196

UNDERSTANDING MEDICAL PAIN MANAGEMENT 202

ACTIVE MANAGEMENT OF THIRD STAGE 208

UNDERSTANDING BREECH BABIES 210

UNDERSTANDING CAESAREAN BIRTHS..212

#4 Checking in – Self-Awareness Exercise. 217

CHAPTER 5 WELCOME 220

Birth Plans and Preferences...220

PREPARING YOUR LABOUR NEST 224

WELCOME – THE FOUR STAGES OF LABOUR 228

#5 Checking in – rating exercise. 237

Recommended Reading: 238

Appendix – Empowerment Through Natural Therapies.....................239

Nutrition...239

Exercise 239

Herbs and Mineral Supplements 240

MASSAGE	241
RELAXATION	243
AROMATHERAPY	243
REFERENCES	246

Welcome

You will find within, a wealth of knowledge, strength and power.

You will learn to trust yourself, your body and nature.

You will have a calm, welcoming birthing.

The techniques and information within this program are your tools, choose those you like, leave those you don't, work with your tools as often as you can.

You will become more proficient with them the more you practice.

Most of all, I hope that you will find a way to 'let go' and enjoy the flow of energy and connection between you and your baby.

Wishing you a safe and very happy Birthing Day!

With metta (loving kindness),

Shari

MY JOURNEY

Becoming a mum has changed me in so many ways; I feel that I am now more the person I am supposed to be than ever before in my adult life. Before finding out that I was pregnant with our son Logan I was very career driven and focused and living, what I now see, as a very masculine lifestyle. I was independent and, in many ways, detached from other people around me.

What has changed is that I now understand the value of connections; family, friends, and especially those very intimate connections between two people and their children. I have also come to understand the value of networks of social support and how to use these to build up resilience for yourself, your family and the community as a whole.

Logan's birth was one of the most amazing days of my life. Sure, it was hard work, but it was most worthwhile! The journey through Logan's pregnancy was a good one, with the help of my husband Ashley I was able to achieve a sense of calmness and relaxation in my life that I don't remember having before. But the real changes started happening after Logan was born, going through postnatal depression and coming out the other side is not something I would wish on anyone but there is most definitely a positive side to it.

This book and the accompanying CD have emerged from this journey in response to my need to feel that I had choices along the way. I realized that I wasn't the only one looking for control; in fact most of the women around me were striving for it in one way or another. The BirthSkills program offers you information about your body, ways of developing awareness of your physical body and techniques to work with it. There are also a variety of techniques that will help you to feel calmer, less fearful and better able to manage the journey from pregnancy to motherhood.

After all of the changes I have been through, I am calmer, I am more resilient, I am more confident within myself and I am more welcoming of others in every way. My journey is not complete thankfully, but I am very grateful for what Logan has bought into my life so far and look forward to what is to come in my life as a mother. I wish this contentment for you too.

My Birthing Stories

I have been blessed with two beautiful births, the first involved some medical intervention and the second was completely natural. I remember feeling very proud and overwhelmed with joy and love on both occasions.

Logan's Birth

Logan's pregnancy was a complete surprise! I had been complaining about feeling dizzy and 'not quite right' for weeks when I woke up one morning with a strong sharp pain in my abdomen. After thinking things through a little I did a pregnancy test just to rule out the possibility…the positive test took both my husband and I completely by surprise and it took us more than a few days to adjust to the idea that we were going to have a baby.

I was prone to being a bit of a control freak at the best of times and the shock of finding out I was more than 8 weeks pregnant sent me into a bit of a spin. My ever calm and wise husband, Ash, suggested that we try some hypnotherapy techniques together to help me relax into the pregnancy. We had learnt enough from our studies in psychology to know that any tension in my body would be having an effect on our growing baby. So at 14 weeks we began practicing relaxation and hypnotherapy at home on a regular basis. I had a wonderful pregnancy, no morning sickness or other complications and like many first time mums, had the luxury of being able to exercise and get regular massage throughout the pregnancy.

By the time I was around 35 weeks pregnant the anxiety had set in again so when strong Braxton Hicks started up at 36 and half weeks I became quite tense with anticipation. I was so eager to see how the birth would go, to find out how I would cope with my body undertaking such an enormous feat. After 10 days of regular Braxton Hicks contractions I went to see my doctor to find out why my labor wasn't becoming established. I was told that I was 4cm open but the stop-start contractions could continue for anything from a few more hours to a couple more weeks. It was also suggested that I was carrying a rather large baby and to prepare myself for a possible emergency caesarean. The thought of a caesarean after two more weeks of contractions was quite unbearable so I opted to be induced hoping that it would increase my chances of a vaginal birth. As it was I was told by a number of different people, both medical and lay, that induction would mean I would definitely need medical pain relief and an episiotomy. So despite the wonderful job my husband had done keeping me calm and relaxed throughout the pregnancy I was now feeling more anxious than ever, however, I also have quite a stubborn streak in me and the more I was told I'd need an epidural the more determined I became to prove that an induced labor doesn't have to be completely medically managed.

We went into the hospital very early on the day I was to be induced, still experiencing the very regular, very strong Braxton Hicks' contractions, but still not in established labor. The induction was fairly straightforward; first the doctor broke my waters then connected up the Syntocinon and started the flow. The labor progressed just as the textbooks said it would, started slow and easy and gradually built up to a stronger more intense feeling. Ash took me through a hypnosis script about 2 hours after the drip was started and I experienced a wonderful endorphin rush after about 20 minutes of deep relaxation, this carried me right through to transition. I focused on my breathing and the midwife got me into a wonderful position up over the top-end of the bed with a stack of pillows supporting my belly. Time passed very strangely and quickly for me, the 8 hours of first stage seemed like only 4 or 5.

During transition I tried to get up to use the bathroom, which turned out to be an awful idea. I experienced about 10-20 minutes of strong pain from the movement out of deep relaxation but once Ash got me into the shower and talked me back into relaxation and the focus on my breathing I was ready to push. Second stage was a little longer than I expected with Logan's head sitting on the perineum (crowning) for over 45 minutes but my doctor was very patient with me, respecting my orders not to perform an episiotomy. However, after 2 hours of pushing and questioning the doctor about why the baby wasn't coming out I demanded an episiotomy and Logan was born in the next contraction!

Logan's birth was quiet, intimate and calm. I felt confident throughout and felt only 10-20 minutes of sharp pain during the 10-hour labour process. Although his birth wasn't 100% intervention-free I felt very proud that I had got through it under my own steam and birthed a beautiful healthy 4.1kg (almost 9 ½lbs) baby boy.

Ebony's Birth

My second baby was even bigger; 4.5kg (10lbs)! Ebony's pregnancy was something I had wanted more than anything in the world and I spent the pregnancy working on my relaxation skills and thinking about how wonderful a completely natural birth was going to be.

At 38 weeks and 4 days we discovered that Ebony was breech, something we had suspected on and off throughout the third trimester but an ultrasound confirmed it for sure. I was booked in for an external cephalic version (ECV) the next day. I spent about an hour that afternoon lying on my bed with a beanbag under my backside to elevate it as high as physically possible, visualising my baby, talking to her and massaging my belly in the direction that I needed her to turn in. I had been quite okay with the idea of birthing my baby in the breech position but it was explained to me that there would be a number of extra onlookers and it wouldn't be the quiet, intimate, birth centre experience I was hoping for, so I focused on turning her. Later that evening my husband took me through the breech turn script using hypnotic techniques to help me focus on and connect with our baby.

When I woke up the next morning I was convinced she had turned but we kept the appointment with the obstetrician for the ECV. After being poked, probed, and pumped full of drugs to prevent the smooth muscle of the uterus contracting (and thus going into labour), as well as prep'd for an emergency caesarean 'just in case', the doctor did a last minute ultrasound to confirm the position of our bub – the moment he paused I knew I was right, we had turned her with our relaxation and hypnotherapy! I have never felt more triumphant!

For some reason, I was convinced through both of my pregnancies that my babies would arrive early, so when Ebony's due day came and went I was a little 'miffed'. I had a wonderful independent midwife looking after me during Ebony's pregnancy and she did a wonderful job keeping me sane through all of my false starts. The strong regular Braxton Hicks surges had started early again, I'd had a show 2 weeks before the expected due date (EDD) and felt ready. However labor didn't start until 12 days after the EDD, once I had made all the physical and emotional preparations for an induction on day 14, had a bit of a panic attack one night about the health of the baby and driven my family crazy with any number of natural methods for bringing on labor – it comes when it comes! My labor started about 9am on a Sunday morning, just as my husband had requested a month or two earlier! We arrived at the birthing centre at around noon and I got straight into the bath. I focused on my breathing and a wonderful visualisation of my son giving me a big hug and kiss got me through the most intense part. When I became restless and felt the urge to push my midwife got me out of the bath. I made it to the end of the bed before the next surge came over me; I leaned over in a standing position and began to bear down. My waters broke with an explosive burst that I didn't know was possible (clearly the midwives knew about this as they managed to jump clear just in time!) and Ebony was born very soon after. The labor had been about 7 hours and despite the sting of sciatica pain shooting down my leg with each surge I managed without medical assistance. Again, I couldn't believe my eyes, here was another baby in my arms which was very obviously (to me anyway!) the most beautiful and wonderful baby to have ever been born! And I had given her a birthday gift of a completely natural, calm and gentle birth.

The journey of pregnancy, birth and motherhood has been an enormous one for me. Through Logan's pregnancy I became highly anxious and was diagnosed with postnatal depression when he was 5 weeks old. It took me until he was almost 3 to feel free of the daily burden of depression and I have fought everyday since to remain calm and compassionate toward myself. As low as I felt after my first birthing experience, I felt even more joyous after my second. Never before in my life have I been happier than being mum to two beautiful children, I have learnt to feel calm despite whatever is going on around me; confident that I have found a place to belong, that I am as good a mum as I can be, and that is good enough; and compassionate towards myself and others, especially other women as we struggle with all of the expectations, pressure and responsibility that today's society places on us, and those we place on ourselves.

INTRODUCTION

This book offers both a philosophy and a toolbox of techniques. It is important that you believe that birth is the process of welcoming your child into the world. You only get this opportunity once with each child and there are things you can do to make this time as wonderful as possible.

There are skills involved in birthing your baby in a calm, positive and welcoming way, skills that have, to a large degree, been lost to many women in modern western society. Skills that in some cultures are passed from mother to daughter or from sister to sister, from aunts and close friends. In an era where elective caesarean is a relatively common option for birthing, many women are handing over the management of their birthings to obstetricians, doctors and other medical personnel. Fear of the unknown leads to relinquishing control and with no one at fault, women find themselves in submissive and vulnerable birthing situations.

Women who are free of fear, who are well informed about the birthing process and their options during the process, who are well supported by an informed partner, who trust their bodies and nature and who are prepared with techniques and skills for creating a positive birthing environment will not find themselves handing over decisions regarding their body or their baby to someone they hardly know. They will be calm, confident and in a good position to make choices that will lead to a positive and welcoming birthing experience for themselves and their baby.

The Philosophy

Philosophy might seem an unusual word to be using with regard to childbirth. The dictionary definition is the secret of truth, the study of science of truths, principles underlying all knowledge or a system of guidance in practical affairs (Collins Concise, 1998).

You may have discovered, since becoming pregnant, that there really is secret women's business! If you are lucky enough, as I was, to find a group of pregnant women who are open and willing to share their remedies for common pregnancy complaints, for passing on helpful information from experienced friends and relatives or from doctors, books or midwives, then you will discover that the truth really is out there! You will also find that there are many versions of the truth and you may need to be very careful in selecting which version suits you best, but with some consideration or by following your developing mother's intuition you will find a 'system of guidance' for yourself.

Your belief system is made up of your accepted truths or reality, things that on a day-to-day basis you do not question. Beliefs guide us in making choices and underlie our behaviour and actions. However, despite having such a strong influence over you, beliefs do not necessarily require evidence or proof for you to accept them. With the right prodding though, you are able to challenge your own beliefs and make an informed decision about whether they really are serving you well.

The skills and techniques offered in this book are evidence-based this means that all of the skills taught have been shown by research to be useful and effective in pregnancy, birthing or for deep relaxation.

The book is based on the belief that all women should have access to the skills and knowledge that will enable them to birth their babies in a calm, confident and welcoming manner. By teaching these skills to a generation of women who are already empowered in other areas of their lives, who are competent at their work, efficient, and in control, hopefully, future generations of women will learn the skills of birthing from their mothers, sisters and friends and their communities will support them in this endeavor.

How to Use This Book

Using these techniques, including self-hypnosis, is not an all or nothing type of thing. It is therefore not a matter of it 'working' or 'not working'. When first learning to meditate or relax deeply, many people have had the experience of thinking "this isn't working, I'm still thinking". At the very least though you are thinking about thinking, you are in the present and you are practicing the skill of meditation or relaxation. Further, your body is still receiving the benefits of your physical relaxation, a state that ideally precedes emotional relaxation.

There are a variety of techniques in this book that you will have the opportunity to learn, some of these you might love, others might not be for you. One of the great things about the book is that you can take what you want from it, what you are ready for, and leave the rest. Something you leave now might be something you come back for later. Choose the techniques and beliefs that are right for you, that fit with other positive aspects of your life and that contribute to your overall feeling of calmness and confidence. Also, if a technique doesn't feel right to you but you like the general idea, feel free to modify it to suit your needs or goals. The things you change or leave out will not be the things that define your birthing experience – only you can do that.

This book will provide you with skills and suggested techniques to enable you to focus on both the positive aspects of the birthing process and the end goal – **healthy mum, healthy baby**.

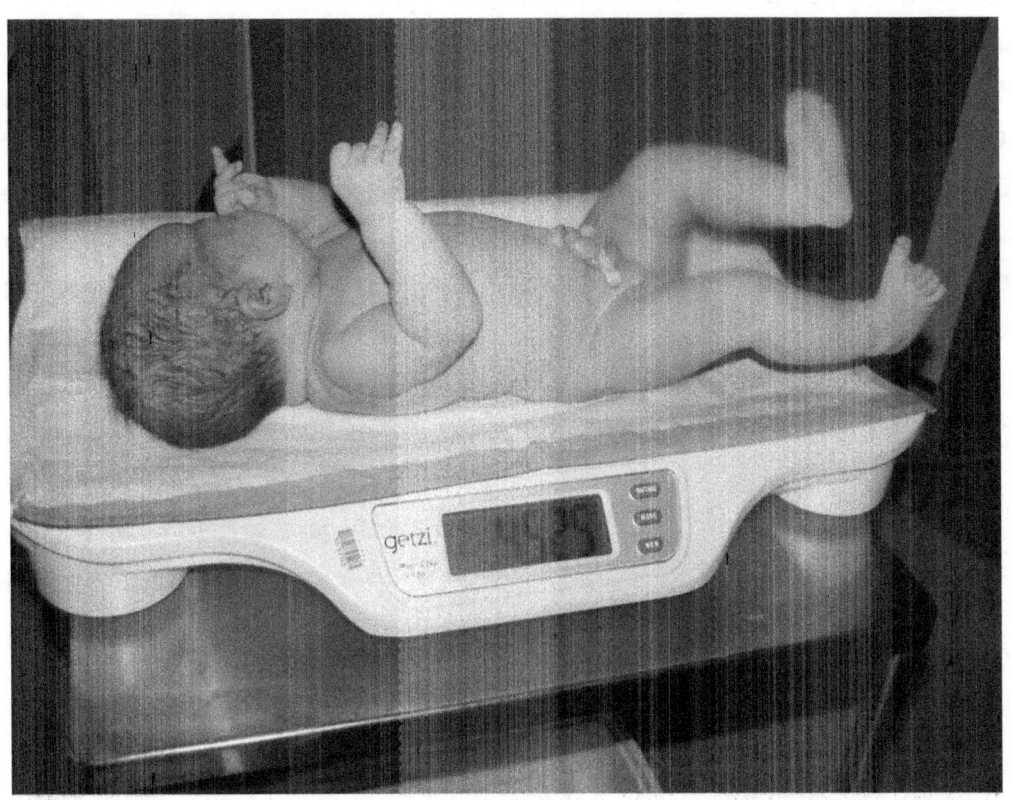

BIRTH STORIES TO INSIPRE

Nicola – Mum to Darcy

As planned Darcy was born at the Birth Centre without any intervention. Labour was so much harder than I could have imagined (especially second stage) but a drug free birth was the first gift I wanted to offer my child and thanks to the hypnosis tools we learned I was able to successfully do it.

I believe our calm birthing experience has had a huge impact on Darcy's development. From the moment he entered world he was very alert. I managed to breastfeed him immediately and he has continued to thrive. Tim and I are so grateful for the knowledge we gained from you. We felt so prepared and never once throughout my long labour (21 hours) did we have any fear.

It makes me happy to know that thanks to you and the BirthSkills classes other women will feel empowered enough to have wonderful birthing experiences and bring into the world calm and happy babies.

> *Hi Shari*
>
> *We just wanted to drop you a quick email to let you know our son, Lachlan arrived in the world at 2:52pm Monday afternoon. The whole experience was fantastic and we used your CD nearly constantly throughout labour. While we fully achieved healthy baby and healthy mum (and proud as punch dad) we also had a completely drug free birth, which was great. Thanks so much for working with us to prepare for this wonderful experience.*
>
> *Jess and Shane - June 2007*

Erika – Mum to Kate

Well, it was all a success! After a 6-hour labour and no drugs or interventions I gave birth to Kate - 8lb 10oz. Shari's BirthSkills course was fantastic. It focused on self-hypnosis or relaxation with affirmations for an empowered birth. There was also a lot of information explaining the whole process and explaining how to remain in control and relaxed at each stage. For the weeks after the course I tried to set aside Daniel's sleep time so that I could go to bed and put on one of Shari's hypnosis CDs - and usually fall asleep! It seemed to work though as I got no blood pressure problems, felt great, and as soon as I put one on in the delivery suite I became relaxed just hearing Shari' voice. I also invested in some essential oils and an electric burner, and made up some massage oils too.

So, at 12.15am on Sunday 16th, the day before she was due, my waters broke. I rang the hospital before 1am to let them know nothing was happening but that I'd be in sometime then went to run the bath. The phone rang - the midwife had checked my file and had to ask me to come in for monitoring because of the c-section last time - but said I might as well have a bath first and get organised! So we got there about

> *Hi Shari*
>
> *We both want to sincerely thank you for teaching us the skills to allow us to have the most wonderful birthing experience, just as we had imagined. We would recommend your course to anyone, and if ever anyone wants to talk to someone who has done the course, then tell them to ring us or email us and we would be happy to tell them about our positive birth experience.*
>
> *Thank you once again*
>
> *Yours sincerely*
>
> *Trent and Lizzie 2006*

2.30am, contractions were irregular and mild, the midwife was one I knew and she let us set up the music and oils and left us to it. She rang the obstetrician at 3.30, he asked her to do an internal and let him know what was happening - I was about 3cm. She told us to order breakfast and lunch as it could be a long day - that it would be about 1cm an hour - like a first labour. Then she left us again and I put the hypnosis CD on and didn't even notice time passing until after 5am. I got up then and had a walk around - and things really started becoming intense. At 6am the OB arrived and put a line in my hand just in case (!!!) and another midwife did a check and said I was about 4cm - but then at 6.30am when the OB checked I was 8cm! He had been planning on just checking on me before going for his Sunday morning walk - he didn't make it out for that!

They got me back on the bed for those checks and monitoring - but after that I couldn't get up because even trying to roll over brought on intense contractions. Another midwife I knew well came in for the birth and both she and the obstetrician were really supportive and positive. Although I was on my back they tried to get me on my side - it just didn't work.

Instead they made sure I wasn't on my tailbone. Unfortunately when she was crowning my body took over and pushed her out - they were trying to slow things down - so she was born at 8.07am, and came straight up onto my chest for a cuddle and feed while I was stitched.

I hope that isn't too much information for you! I'm certain that confidence plays a huge part in going through with a VBAC. Several friends who have had 2 c-sections have told me they feel they "chickened out" or similar. I am amazed though at how many people ask me which I would choose now having done both! I really still only see the c-section as an emergency option.

Erika – Luka Ewan

Am writing to let you know that my little boy Luka was born last week. Labour was 10 hours in total (5 of which were spent at home), and he arrived weighing a healthy 7.3 pounds.

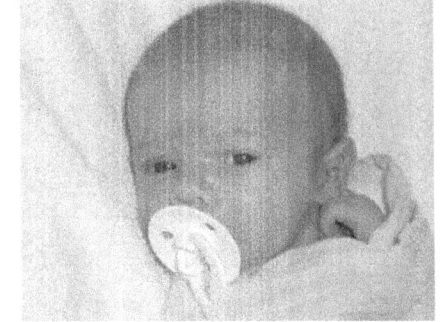

My birthing experience was everything I had hoped for (thanks in part to your guidance), with no intervention, and I was able to escape without any stitches - think the perineal massage definitely helped there. I was even able to have a physiological third stage, which I had hoped for. Luka attached to the breast straight away and I haven't had any problems so far with breast-feeding.

Am at home now enjoying getting to know my little man. Am still feeling quite hormonal and everything is still very surreal but am taking it one day at a time.

Michelle – Eli Terence

Eli arrived last Saturday (12 days early - as we suspected he might be!). The birth went really well with about 6 hours of early stage labour (which I didn't realise was happening for a while) and 7 hours of established labour. We got to the hospital at 2.30pm where they told us I was already fully dilated and Eli was born at 5pm - a drug free experience! Pretty amazing stuff.

I used lots of breathing that you had gone through with us and spent most of the time on all fours visualising that I was blowing a forest over with my out breaths! Andrew was my rock during labour and I couldn't have done it without him.

We spent 5 nights in hospital as Eli has jaundice and had to spend 36 hours under light therapy. Since coming home on Thursday everything has been pretty smooth sailing and he appears to be a lighter shade of yellow as each day passes. I am coping Ok with the sleep deprivation and those moments of 'oh my god I have no idea what I am doing!' and just taking it moment by moment. Your rapid relaxation technique has been a godsend in helping me get to sleep quickly for those power naps and to clear the mind

Diane – Jack William

Jack William, arrived 2 weeks early, weighing 7lb and 9½oz. I am really pleased – and proud to say that the birth was totally drug and intervention free.

My waters broke the night before – which was a bit of a shock, but I had a bit of a show the day before so thought that maybe things would happen sooner rather than later. Unlike my fear of the actual moment, the drive to the hospital, which was around 30 – 40 minutes away, did not happen in rush hour, I was not in any pain and lots of the lights were green!! We had a very nice run up there, chatting about what was going to happen, baby

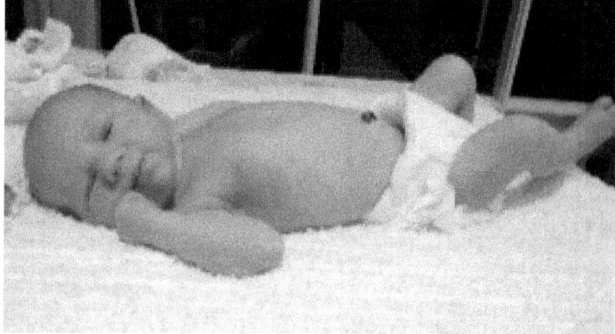

names etc – it was lovely. At the hospital I was hooked up to a machine and was having contractions but couldn't feel them. We both stayed in a room overnight and I got to sleep around 11pm. At 1am I woke as I was now feeling contractions, however I just kept sleeping through them, breathing and going to the loo every so often as sitting there seemed to be more comfortable at times than lying. I decided not to time them or get hung up on time and how long it was taking, just go with the flow and do what my body wanted to do. At 7-7.30 am the nurse came to wake me up and I walked through to the Birthing Suite and was pretty sure that I was quite far along as I felt sweaty but cold and just a bit odd, which I think was actually transition. When I got to the Birthing Suite the midwife examined me for the first time and couldn't believe I was actually nearly fully dilated! All my plans for massages etc went out the window, as all I was really concentrating on was breathing, relaxing and some visualization. The midwife was amazed that while checking the baby's heartbeat, lying flat on the bed, I had a really large contraction, and was so relaxed, but it actually felt easier lying down than standing, maybe because I have done yoga and relaxation exercises mainly lying on my back. The obstetrician arrived and I decided to be on my knees at the side of the bed, leaning towards my husband, who was holding my hands. The midwife and obstetrician were sitting on the floor. I don't know how long I pushed for, it didn't seem like anytime at all, and out came Jack at 10am, 9 hours after I felt the first contraction– crying almost before he got out! I had my music playing, which was about the only thing I did manage to use! It was all very peaceful and relaxing, I didn't really say much to anyone, except to tell them when a contraction was coming – there was no screaming, swearing or shouting at anyone. I was really surprised at myself and how I coped as the pain didn't seem nearly as bad as I thought it would be, I am so pleased that I did the BirthSkills course and learnt more about the body and not to fight the pain, I think that really helped me.

Paula - Santino

The breathing & visualization got us through 30 hours of contractions.

Rossano had two weekends of work so we were counting the days anxiously so that they wouldn't clash. Luckily when Rossano got home at 6.00 pm on that Saturday night after the last wedding is when my contractions started. First at seven minutes apart for the first hour and then straight into five minutes. This is where they stayed for the next 26 hours or so. We found walking brought them closer together so we did lots of that. The last hour saw the contractions a minute apart with them cascading over each other.

I only had one moment of weakness where I started to get anxious on the Sunday afternoon while we were still at home but once we went into the hospital and we were walking around the hospital grounds I found I was able to get back into my breathing and visualization without any apprehension whatsoever. Having seen the labour ward on a previous hospital visit allowed me to visualize that area weeks before and prepare.

The midwife we had at the hospital during the birth was wonderful and was very supportive of our techniques as was our OB. He was due to be away for the weekend but came down early to be with us. Not once was there any mention of drugs or pain relief and they allowed me to use our techniques. At around 10.30/11.00 pm Sunday evening we commenced the pushing stage & again I was able to use what you taught us through this. Our OB did have to artificially rupture my membranes and after one hour of pushing, it appeared the baby still wasn't able to come out. Our OB tried to ease the baby out with forceps using my contractions to guide him. This was the first time in 30 hours that I had to have any medication and this was to numb the area. After two attempts our OB made the call to do an emergency caesarean as I was starting to hemorrhage. Our baby through this whole time was fine, his heat rate was strong and did not waiver.

Once our OB made the call to do the emergency caesarean it all happened very fast. Within five minutes we were on our way up to the operating theatre. There was another woman due to have a caesarean but they were able to postpone her and I was able to use her whole team i.e. anesthesiologist and pediatrician etc. Again all during this time I was still in a wonderful place and certainly not feeling distressed or anxious. Even while in the operating theatre & the OB was actually doing the incision I remember talking to Rossano & was overjoyed at the arrival of our baby and even planning the next one.

The next baby will need to be caesarean again but I do not feel in any way that I missed out on any birth experience or bonding with my baby.

All the techniques that we had learnt came in handy too especially with the recovery of the caesarean. The OB and midwives couldn't believe my recovery and the ability to be walking around by that afternoon after Santino's safe delivery at 12.36 am Monday morning. My use of medication was only during the caesarean i.e. the epidural and drips etc that they gave me and a total of about four Panadol in the week after to assist with the pain relief.

We are now getting so much enjoyment out of our baby and every day brings new and exciting things. Also your techniques have taught me to fall asleep really fast so that you make the most of the sleep that you do get!!

Kirstin – Alison

Alison was born at 8:39am on 11 May. My membranes ruptured the day before but because she was so low she was sort of acting like a cork and I wasn't really sure if it really was amniotic fluid so I went to the hospital in the afternoon and the midwife confirmed that that was what it was. They wanted me to stay in the hospital after that but I wanted to go home so that's what we did. The ob told me that I had to check into the hospital at 2am on Friday morning at the latest if I wanted to get a private room because they were really full so I agreed. They said that they would have to induce if labour hadn't started within 18 hours but I didn't worry too much about that because I was sure that it wouldn't be necessary.

Marcus and I went home, did more relaxation exercises, had dinner and went to bed. At about 11:30 I woke up with contractions. I slept a little bit more and eventually got up. Marcus did the massage you showed us, and I also had a shower. At 2am on Friday we went to the hospital, and they took us to our room (which was great - double bed and our own shower and toilet - luxury!). Marcus dimmed the lights, put on your relaxation CDs, did more massage, countless trips to the microwave to heat up hot packs and really helped me through the contractions. Because the hospital was so busy, the midwives left us alone and we got on with things in peace, just like we had planned. I was really comfortable and calm throughout this time, and very focused on my breathing. At about 5:30 I really needed to push, so Marcus buzzed a midwife. It took ages before one came (maybe not that long but it felt like a long time). They put me in a wheelchair and wheeled me to the delivery room, and the whole time I was still focusing on my breathing. In the delivery room the midwife had a look (first time since we checked into the hospital) and said that I was

10cm and could start pushing. Marcus and I were so happy that we reached that stage all by ourselves without any interference.

I pushed for three hours but my contractions had slowed down a lot (only getting 2 every ten minutes). Because the contractions were so slow, the augmented them with synctocinon, but even that didn't work so well. Towards the end, I had nothing left to give and I ran out of puff completely and didn't think I could go on. Marcus was so encouraging but I think this part of the labour was pretty traumatic for him. I must have tried to climb off the bed because they strapped my legs down! After three hours I had enough and yelled at the ob to "suck it out!" and that's what he did.

Alison was vacuumed out and I had a second-degree tear, but the vacuum was only on her head for one push so she didn't get that funny shape on her head and her apgar was 9 and 9 so she was fine. My plan for the third stage was to do it without intervention but because of the lack of contractions I needed the intervention but by that stage I couldn't care less. Alison was out and that was all that mattered.

She is a really fantastic baby - she's hardly every cranky and has a very happy nature. I'm getting used to the broken sleep, and also have breastfeeding under control (this was much harder than I thought it would be).

Marcus and I are SO glad because we achieved the kind of birth that we were hoping for (i.e. drug free, healthy baby, one where we were in control of what was happening - for most of it!).

If I hadn't learnt the techniques, I wouldn't have been confident enough to put my foot down and go home when they wanted to admit me to hospital when my membranes ruptured, and we probably also wouldn't have managed the first stage of labour as well as we did. The second stage didn't go exactly the way we wanted it to, but it was only 3 hours and things turned out OK so we are even happy about how that part went!

Nyaree – Stella Jean

I finally have the chance to sit down at the computer so I wanted to email you to let you know that we have had our baby!

Her name is Stella Jean. She was born at 0005 on 19th November (right on time!), weighing 7lbs 12 oz and was 51.5cm in length.

The birth went really well and was a lovely experience. I woke up at 5am on the 18th and my membranes had ruptured and I had a show. I rang the hospital and they said to have a shower, eat breakfast etc then come on in. So we remained very calm, packed our bags, made arrangements for the pets and drove to the hospital. By the time we got there I was having surges every 3-5 minutes for 30-45 seconds. They were not too intense so I was able to breathe through them nicely. For the next few hours at the hospital they were pretty busy so we were pretty much left to it so we set up the room with my oils and crystals etc and walked around the park, listened to music and just generally relaxed.

By the time they checked me that afternoon, I was 3-4cm and doing fine. Over the next couple of hours the surges became more intense and lasting longer. I had a bath, which helped for a while and did some more walking.

By 5pm ish I was really starting to feel uncomfortable and was finding it difficult to keep breathing properly. They checked me again and I was still only 4cm. My OBGYN recommended that we have the oxytocin drip to get things moving, as it had already been 12 hours, he also suggested that I have an epidural as I was already very tired and uncomfortable (at this point I did not want to leave the toilet, it was really quite funny!). After thinking it over for a while we both decided that this would be best so that I could be more relaxed and refreshed to meet our baby.

So by 6.30-7pm I was much more comfortable and able to get some rest. The breathing also helped me here with my fear of needles - I didn't flinch once while they gave me the local, epidural & inserted the IV drip!

My OBGYN returned around 11.40pm to check on me by which time the epidural had worn off a lot and I was feeling the surges again, and we were ready to go! We gave birth to her about 15 minutes later, which was absolutely amazing - I watched it all in a mirror, and the atmosphere was quiet, calm and loving. She came out alert and calm, she received high AGPAR scores as well and fed straight away, it was absolutely an awesome experience!

I am really glad we did your course and I believe that the relaxation & breathing techniques helped - with a little more practice we could have probably done without the epidural, but I do not have any regrets, only very happy memories. I also think we were very lucky that my doctor and the midwife were supportive and respected our wishes - they even thanked us for such a lovely experience! We were the talk of the hospital for our stay too as there were only 2 normal deliveries that week, and we had a lot of midwives come in to meet us and congratulate us on doing such a good job. One midwife even said that we restored her faith in natural childbirth.

One More Birthing Story...

You might remember in 2000, a woman climbing a tree to escape raging floodwaters in Mozambique. The main reason you might remember this is because the woman gave birth in the tree. I have a very vivid memory of watching the news footage with my own mum and asking if women can give birth in a tree, with no-one to help and no pain relief, why all the fuss that women in our society seem to need? My mum said that she guessed if things are going well, we don't need the hospitals and medication and so on, we just think we do.

Photos BBC News 2000.

Baby born in Mozambique treetop as floodwaters swirl
Thursday, March 2, 2000

By MIKE COHEN

THE ASSOCIATED PRESS

Excerpt - MAPUTO, Mozambique -- Floods forced about 1 million people from their homes in Mozambique, but even they cannot stop other forces of nature: A woman gave birth yesterday to a baby girl in a treetop where she had lived above raging water for four days. An hour later, Sophia Pedro and her daughter were rescued after a medic winched down from a helicopter to cut the newborn's umbilical cord. The dramatic rescue came as thousands more Mozambicans remain stranded in trees, on rooftops or on shrinking spits of land.

Pedro, 26, and her newborn daughter Rositha were among 915 people plucked from the floodwaters in central Mozambique yesterday by South African military helicopters. Rositha was born as a rescue helicopter hovered overhead and began hoisting the eight occupants of the tree to safety. Helicopter pilot Chris Berlyn said crew-member Stewart Back had been lowered into the tree and discovered that Pedro was about to give birth. He said the child was born two minutes later. Berlyn raced back to a base camp to pick up Godfrey Nongovela, a medic. Nongovela and other crew managed to get the woman and child aboard the helicopter. "We took them to Chibuto, where the police took them to a clinic," Berlyn said. Nurses fussed over Rositha and said the baby appeared to be doing absolutely fine.

It might be an interesting exercise for you to use the following scale periodically as you make your way through this manual and practice relaxation. This scale will help you chart your journey of self-awareness and reveal how practicing the techniques in this book will alter your levels of calmness and confidence.

Thinking about labour and birthing, on a scale from 0 to 100, where 0 represents not at all and 100 means completely, how would you rate yourself <u>right now</u> in terms of:

0 _____ 100
CONFIDENCE

0 _____ 100

CALMNESS

Place a mark on the lines above to indicate how you feel <u>right now</u>

Thinking about labour and birthing, on a scale from 0 to 100, where 0 represents not at all and 100 means completely, how would you <u>want to feel during labour and birthing</u> in terms of:

0 _____ 100

CONFIDENCE

0 _____ 100

CALMNESS
Place a mark on the lines above to indicate how you <u>want to feel during labour and birthing</u>

The only thing that can affect your birthing experience is your belief system. What you believe, you will find: if you believe that birthing will be a painful and traumatic experience you will most likely interpret the sensations you will feel accordingly. Alternatively, if you believe that birthing is a natural process and that women's bodies were designed to do it, then you will be much more likely to interpret the workings of the uterus in a similar manner to the workings of other muscles in your body – but with one obviously different and wonderful outcome – the birth of your baby.

If you go into labour and the birthing process looking for pain – you will most likely find it. If you go in to labour looking to work cooperatively with your body in the wonderful process of birthing your baby, you will find joy in every surge as each one brings you closer to holding your baby.

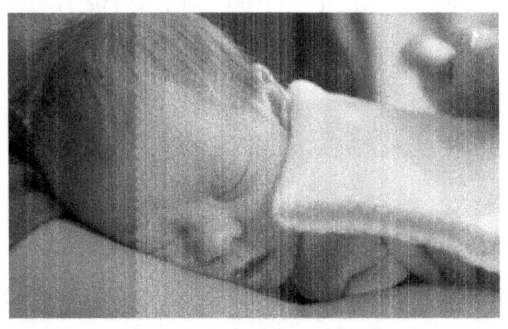

CHAPTER 1 AWARENESS

I will addresses awareness in a number of ways. There are a number of reasons that awareness is so very important with regard to birthing and parenting. Awareness allows you to take control of things previously uncontrollable; for example, the fear associated with someone else's birthing experience. You might be quite surprised at how much more calm and confident you feel simply after becoming aware of some of the external and internal influences on your beliefs about birthing.

A few things that you will find it useful to be aware of:

- your beliefs;
- what you are focused on;
- what and who you trust;
- the choices you have;
- how your body works during labour;
- your goals and desired outcomes; and
- how you would like to welcome your baby.

Grantly Dick-Read during his early training asked the question "What's wrong with labour?" and after 35 years of obstetric practice he came up with some very interesting answers which have served as the underpinnings of the techniques in this book.

Beliefs

In his research, obstetrician Dr Grantly Dick-Read went back about 6,000 years to the period when Druids were around. At that time mothers were somehow connected to the deity and it was believed that they could bring forth a child at will. Research suggests that the people of the time hadn't connected intercourse with conception. Birth was viewed as a celebration of life. When a mother was giving birth the family gathered around and participated in a spiritual celebration. This belief about birth existed for many years and the Grecian philosophers and fathers of medicine, Hypocrites and Aristotle wrote very positive descriptions of birth. Hypocrites observed that nature was the best physician and should not be interfered with unnecessarily. Sorannas, an obstetrician of the times, collated many of the ancient writings together, none of which referred to pain or discomfort during childbirth, except in special circumstances. There was some mention of complications and the herbs and brews that were used to bring the mother into relaxation in order to calm the problem, similar to modern day anesthetics. The overriding belief about birth during these times was that it was to be welcomed and celebrated (Dick-Read, 1945).

According to Dick-Read's research there was a shift in prevailing beliefs, when Judo Christianity took over Pagan civilization and replaced the teachings of the gods and goddesses with the belief in a single male god. The religious authorities of the time had a great deal of power and could dictate to the medical physicians, banning them from attending labouring mothers. Mothers were often left alone in childbirth without any help, midwives were often persecuted as witches and only shepherds or herdsmen were permitted to tend to the newborn baby . It was believed by the church people that childbirth was a 'burden' that women should bear as punishment for the sins of Eve in the Garden of Eden.

The Christian Bible, in the Book of Genesis, tells the story of Adam and Eve. Dr Dick-Read suggests that these cultural beliefs are perhaps partly responsible for some of the fear surrounding childbirth in contemporary society. Quoting the book of Genesis, when Adam and Eve were asked to leave the garden, God said to the woman "I will greatly multiply your pain in childbearing; in pain you shall bring forth children" (Genesis 3:16).

According to Dick-Read, the Christian belief system is responsible for the perceptions of childbirth present in Western civilization. An interesting thing about this is that when the Hebrew word for pain is used in other parts of the scripture it is not intended to mean pain, it is intended to mean hard work, labour. Yet, in the story of Genesis it has been interpreted as physical pain.

Some believe there was a corruption in the translation but whether this is true or not, the interpretation has been passed from generation to generation. Because the church was so powerful during Pagan times they were able to decree that only a live child would be taken, if a mother was in complicated labour they would do a caesarean with no anesthetic, the baby was born but often died because there was no knowledge of hygiene. The mother was usually left to die but her soul was saved because she delivered another soul into the world.

Medicine took on a renewed authority during the 16th and 17th centuries and many compassionate people attended to mothers and babies. The work of Sorannas was rediscovered but still not a lot was known about hygiene. A doctor named Semelweis who observed statistics wrote that 30% of the mothers who died did so after the doctors had attended them in childbirth but only 3% died after the midwives attended. What was the difference? He noticed that the midwives washed their hands. The doctors would be working down in the morgue where bodies were beginning to decompose and bacteria forming and then without washing their hands, attend a mother in childbirth. Because it is such a vascular area and during childbirth, a vulnerable area, infection easily passed into the women's bodies and both mothers and babies died. It took 40 years of hospital birthing before Florence Nightingale suggested that anyone who attended a birthing mother should wash his or her hands first.

In the 1840's anesthetics were discovered, initially nobody wanted to give chloroform or ether to the labouring mother because they didn't know if it might harm the baby. There was also a group of people who clung to the belief system that stipulated "God should not be deprived from the cries of women in labour". Belief systems are extremely powerful.

If you believe that birth is painful do you know why you hold that belief? Because that's what everybody has told you and perhaps you have had a previous experience that provides you with strong evidence? Dr Grantly Dick-Read extensively examined what was wrong with labour, particularly in Western Society. He believed that superstition, civilization and culture brought influences to bear on the minds of women, influences that introduced justifiable fears. This was, and still is, a large part of the problem. Fear of childbirth has been passed on from generation to generation and it has become etched in the minds of young women and mothers-to-be. Little girls are exposed to all kinds of horror stories about childbirth through overhearing their mother's conversations, being told directly about a traumatic experience or watching birthing portrayed on television or movies. As a child you listened to it in the background, but covertly it left an impression in your mind, and contributed to the beliefs you have come to hold about birthing. Now you're approaching your own birth experience and quite possibly, people keep telling you about their horrible birth stories and your mind goes back, recalling all the other scenarios you've heard about or experienced over the years.

After all of this, by the time they are approaching the birthing of their baby many women are in quite a state of fear and tension.

Because of the powerful effect the mind has on the body, these beliefs can be quite detrimental to your birthing preparations, and for many women, to birthing itself. Dr Grantly Dick-Read termed this process the Fear-Tension-Pain-Syndrome. The more frightened you are, the more tense you become, and the stress hormones send the body into fight or flight. Instead of the woman's blood and oxygen resources being sent to the uterus where they are needed, they are being directed to the extremities for running or fighting, leaving the uterus, and your baby, deprived of blood and oxygen.

So, the problem isn't with labour itself, it's with the socialization that we receive, the imprinting of negative expectations about childbirth and the lack of proper preparation and instruction during our pregnancies.

Some prenatal classes tend to play up all of the things that could go wrong, because of litigation healthcare professionals need to cover themselves for any risks involved in the processes and procedures they use. Rather than birthing classes, many of these types of sessions have become information evenings about drugs, medication and medical procedures. Further reinforcing the expectation that birthing is a horrible, traumatic process that requires medical intervention as a matter of routine. As a result, many women see labour as something that is wrong and needs to be fixed.

However, if as a society, we hold the belief that with proper guidance and preparation mothers and fathers can understand how the birthing body works, we are then in a position to teach the techniques and skills that once used to come naturally, that rightly should be passed from mother to daughter – that people shouldn't have to pay for, they should just 'know'.

DR GRANTLY DICK-READ – **author of *Childbirth Without Fear***

Dr Dick-Read's (1889-1959) true interest in birthing began in 1913. In his latter years, he said he often remembered his experience with a woman in White chapel whose name he'd long forgotten before he realized the far-reaching effect she had on him by a casual remark during her birthing. In 1913 Dick-Read rode his pushbike to where she lived. There were a lot of babies born in the hospital where he worked, but many babies in Britain at the time were born at home. The doctor arrived around 2am to her home and he said it was very evident of the poverty of this place. He later wrote that despite these poverty stricken surroundings there was a calmness, a kindliness, and a peacefulness in the atmosphere. Eventually the baby was born without a great deal of fuss and with no intervention, the only disruption in the process was when the mother got to second stage and Dick-Read took the lid off the ether bottle (because that was the practice in those days), she just said no, "no thank you". He stepped back and watched while this mother brought her baby into the world without any drama, no fuss and with very little discomfort.

This must have been the first time Grantly Dick-Read had ever seen what he later called a normal birth. He was used to the hospital where he talked about mothers who were screaming in agony and there was a very common theme of using chloroform, ether and forceps as a matter of routine.

A short time after the birth of her baby, Dick-Read asked the White chapel mother why she didn't take the drugs for the pain, according to his story she didn't answer at once. She looked up at the laywoman, the midwife, and then she looked out the window to the breaking dawn. She turned to Doctor Dick-Read and said "It didn't hurt, it wasn't meant to was it doctor?" She obviously had a very different expectation of birth than the mothers who he had been looking after in hospital. For weeks and months afterwards he puzzled about this birth. That sentence kept drumming back into his ears – "it didn't hurt, it wasn't meant to was it?".

Dr Dick- Read began to ask whether the experience of labour was responsible for the emotional state of the mother or if the emotional state of the mother was actually responsible for the experience of labour?

In asking this question he discovered two very important things:

- **that fear creates tension, tension creates catecholamine (stress hormones), and these hormones (the body's chemical messengers) help to facilitate the transportation of pain messages from the body to the brain; and**
- **there's nothing wrong with labour – it is the way western society approaches labour that creates fear, which leads to tension and results in unnecessary pain.**

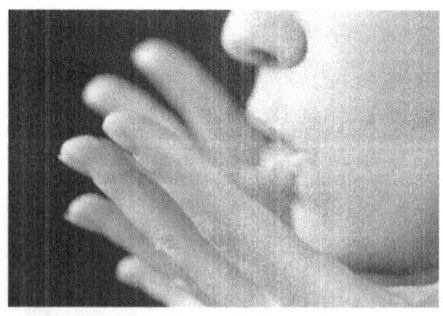

THE FEAR/TENSION/PAIN SYNDROME

In 1914 Grantly Dick-Read went to war as a medical officer in the army and had the opportunity to witness mothers from other cultures birthing their babies. He wrote about mothers birthing their babies, seemingly with no discomfort or pain, in trenches or whatever safe place they could find.

Dick-Read was injured in the war by shrapnel and had a severe back wound, and in a very intimate way he learned about pain. It was during this experience that he came to understand the relationship between Fear, Tension, and Pain and how our beliefs interact with this sensory experience.
He started to think that the belief system played a huge part in the outcome of birth, so he began to examine the belief system in greater detail.

Something else that was happening at the same time in the scientific community was the investigation into anatomy and physiology, particularly into the role that the autonomic nervous system plays in many bodily functions, soon Dr Dick-Read began to discover how much it played out in the birth of a baby.

An easy way to understand how the automatic part of the autonomic nervous system works is to think about when you get a fright. Your heart starts to beat faster as your mind alerts your body and immediately there is more blood pumped to your arms and legs to get you ready for whatever action you need to take for survival – this is known as the 'fight or flight' response. During this experience the body produces a group of hormones called catecholamines (including adrenaline and cortisol), the stress hormones, which maintain the alertness in your mind and body. When these hormones are running through your body you are ready for action, tense, alarmed and unable to relax.

You might like to think about two different rooms to help you understand how the fear/tension/pain syndrome leads to a negative birthing experience.

The Busy Room represents the state that your body is in when the fight or flight response has been activated. The Relaxation Room is the opposite of this.

If a labouring mother spends most of her first stage in the Busy Room she uses a lot of energy, she quickly becomes tired and exhausted. Her arms and legs will use up the deeply oxygenated blood and her uterus will be relatively deprived of the resources it needs during labour to work efficiently, this can be when babies go into distress and medical intervention is required to ensure safe delivery.

The Busy Room

This is busy, there's lots of noise, bright light and hurried movement.

The Relaxation Room

This is calm, peaceful and just right for relaxing in.

> **Example of how Fear leads to Tension:**
>
> *Personally, I don't like spiders. If someone refers to a spider being in close proximity to me or describes a spider in some detail I find myself tensing up, my shoulders and fists become tight and my legs become prepared for running. My fear of spiders leads to tension in my muscles.*

THE FIGHT OR FLIGHT RESPONSE

To our cave-dwelling ancestors, the fight or flight response was an essential tool for survival, which evolved over many thousands of years living in wild and dangerous places. To us, in today's relatively civilised society, it is often an ineffective response, which can actively prevent us from responding usefully to a situation.

The flight or fight response, also called the "acute stress response", was first described by Walter Cannon in 1929. The theory states that animals react to threats with a general discharge of the sympathetic nervous system. In general terms, an animal has two options when faced with danger. They can either face the threat ("fight"), or they can avoid the threat ("flight").

The fight or flight response begins once something is perceived as a threat, or potential threat. The primitive parts of the brain then send a message to the adrenal glands, which begins a process involving a number of hormones including adrenaline, whose purpose is to prepare the body for vigorous emergency action.

The main changes that occur in your body as a result of the fight or flight response are:

- Non-survival processes are immediately switched off. In particular, if the body is digesting food, that is stopped immediately, and you may notice a feeling of churning of 'butterflies' in the stomach, or feeling nauseous or you may actually be sick.

  More importantly, the uterus is not a part of your defense system and will be relatively deprived of the resources it needs to work effectively (i.e. blood and oxygen) it will not be switched off as long as your body is also releasing oxytocin, but it will not be working as well as it could be, prolonging labour and contributing to your feeling fatigued and uncomfortable.

- The liver releases glucose into the bloodstream. Fats are released into the bloodstream from the fat stores in the body. These are fuel for the muscles, so oxygen is needed to burn them - so shallow breathing starts and the rate of breath increases, and you will begin to feel breathless and perhaps light-headed as a result.

  Having Fuel and oxygen in the bloodstream, the body needs to get it to the muscles as soon as possible - (remember, the body thinks this is a life or death emergency). So to pump the blood quickly, the heart begins beating far faster and blood pressure rises (not good during pregnancy or labour).

  With an increase in heart rate the sweat glands start to produce more sweat as the body seeks to dissipate the heat that will be generated by the vigorous muscular activity for which the body is preparing, thus increasing the chances of becoming dehydrated.

-The immune system decreases resistance to disease and infection.

- In preparation for instant action, muscle tension increases, and the person may notice shaking, or restlessness. If the response goes on for long enough, chronic headaches or backache may result and you will become easily fatigued. Furthermore, the muscular tension around the uterus will impede its action.

As all of this is happening in the body, there are two important changes in the brain's neurology.

- First, reflexes are speeded up. At the same time, so is the thinking, and some people notice scattered, unfocused thoughts leading to further anxiety and panic.

- Second, the blood supply to the frontal parts of the brain, responsible for higher levels of reasoning is reduced, while the blood supply to the more primitive parts, near the brain stem, is increased.

These parts of the brain are responsible for automatic and impulsive decision making and behaviour, and a person in fight or flight mode may be prone to impulsive thinking and behaviour as the more rational part of the brain has been effectively 'switched off' – this is not a good state to be in if a choice regarding an emergency situation needs to be made. When you are in a relaxed state, you have control over the 'switch' to your frontal lobes and can use your relaxation techniques to turn this part of the brain on and off at will - in fight or flight, the sympathetic nervous system takes over control of this 'switch' leaving the person panicked and less likely to make good decisions.

Some psychologists suggest that we lose up to 30 IQ points in situations of extreme stress!

Also, the areas of the brain around the brain stem are responsible for receiving pain messages and the increased blood flow will contribute to the perception and interpretation of pain, meaning that women in labour who are operating in the fight or flight mode will experience more pain than those who are calm and relaxed.

For the unprepared labouring woman, the body's responses in fight or flight mode are automatic and out of conscious control. However, once you have learnt about how the body works during labour and what you can do to contribute to the effectiveness of the birthing process, these responses can be brought under control and used to your advantage.

HOW FEAR AFFECTS LABOUR

Having just read about how the fight or flight response affects the body, you might now be able to get a sense of how the changes that occur inhibit and impede the process of birthing. For example, when a labouring woman becomes frightened and anxious and goes into 'fight or flight' the body sends the rich oxygenated blood to the arms and legs ready for hitting or running, whatever action is needed for survival. This leaves the uterus working under difficult conditions.

Fear and tension create the following working environment for the uterus:

The uterus (a muscle just like the bicep or thigh muscle) is left relatively starved of blood and oxygen. Like any other muscle, the uterus needs oxygen to work effectively. **If the uterus doesn't have the oxygen it needs to contract as well as possible each time, labour is likely to take longer.**

The tension created by the fight or flight response means that the uterus muscle has to contract against other muscles, which are tense, forcing it against tightness and leaving less room for the movement of the contractions. **If the uterus is forced against tight abdominal or pelvic muscles the pressure created is likely to be perceived as pain.** Further, the baby is forced down against tight muscles, creating even more discomfort.

A woman labouring in fight or flight mode might also find that her baby goes into distress during labour. If your uterus is relatively deprived of oxygen as a result of the deviated blood supply, your baby is likely to also experience this deprivation, on top of this your baby receives all of the stress hormones produced by your body and experiences the corresponding physiological changes, increased heart rate, increased blood pressure, increased need for oxygen (which is not available). If your baby shows signs of being in distress during labour it becomes much more likely for medical intervention to be required to ensure your baby is delivered quickly and safely.

The uterus is connected directly to the sympathetic nervous system; the system responsible for the 'fight or flight' response. Animals, including humans, can stop their labour if there is danger. As a survival mechanism, this is good, as a conditioned response to the sight or smell of a hospital corridor, this is not helpful. Often, when a fearful or anxious mother, who has been labouring beautifully at home, arrives at the hospital, her labour appears to stop. This pause or 'failure to progress', a response to the mother's fear, is often a signal to hospital staff to offer medical techniques to get labour going again. For an unprepared mother, these techniques can result in a more intense birthing experience, resulting in the woman asking for pain medication and in turn handing over control of her body and her birthing.

In response to Dr Dick-Read's question *"What's wrong with labour?"*, the answer seems to be, a lack of understanding about birthing; our belief systems; and a lack of preparation during pregnancy. We must accept that there will always be a certain percentage of mothers who will need assistance during their births in order for them to reach their goal of **healthy mum, healthy baby**. However, many more women than at present would be able to give birth naturally if they had the opportunity, like you do now, to understand what happens during labour to and to learn the skills to work with the process.

Use this space to record any fears or concerns you have about birthing your baby. You can come back after working through the book to see if these worries are still relevant closer to when your baby is due to be born. You may find that you will have developed new skills for dealing with these concerns.

THE PROCESS – PART 1: HOW THE UTERUS WORKS

Did you know that the uterus is primarily a muscle??? I knew more about episiotomies and epidurals than the working of the uterus when I first became pregnant....

It is very important that you understand how your body will work during labour so that you may work with it. The uterus is an amazing piece of machinery and is not fully understood by researchers or even obstetricians.

We do know that the uterus was designed specifically to grow and birth a baby. And just like you didn't need to consciously think about and grow your baby's liver or legs, you do not need to consciously think about using your uterus. When it comes time to birth your baby, your uterus will know what do to, even if it has never done this before. However, if you understand what the muscle is doing you will be able to interpret and respond to the corresponding sensations appropriately, you will also be able to use helpful visualizations and thoughts to work with the muscle layers of the uterus.

The uterus is composed of 3 tissue layers, the outer layer is called the parametrium, the inner layer is the myometrium and the innermost layer is the endometrium (responsible for nurturing the placenta during pregnancy but when not pregnant this is the lining of the uterus that is shed each month and responsible for menstrual bleeding). The middle layer of the uterus, the **myometrium**, is most important to the birthing process and is made up of 3 layers of smooth involuntary muscle:

The Structure of the Uterus:

Outer longitudinal layer

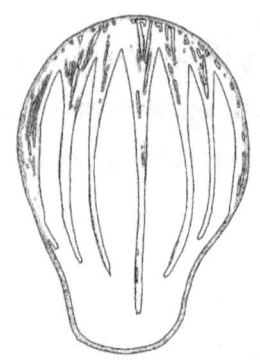

These fibers run vertically up and down the length of your abdomen and work to pull the cervix (which has become very soft and stretchable during the final days of pregnancy) up and open. Under the influence of the naturally produced chemical messenger called oxytocin these muscle layers draw the inner circular fibers upward during the first stage of labour to create the opening or dilation of the cervix (the neck or opening of the uterus). With each contraction or surge, this layer of muscle tightens and shortens to draw the inner layer up around your baby's head, just like putting on a roll-neck jumper or skivvy, but upside down!

The outer layer of muscle does most of its work during the first stage, the part where the cervix is being drawn open (or dilating), to open the uterus far enough for your baby to pass through and into the vaginal path.

Middle layer

This layer of muscle is interwoven with blood vessels. Its precise function is ensuring blood is distributed throughout the uterus. This layer of muscle is also responsible for closing off the blood vessels of the placenta after birth and which in turn allows the placenta to come away from the wall of the uterus be birthed or expelled. In order for the uterus to function as it is designed to, this layer needs a strong, continuous supply of blood, enough for both the working muscles and your baby.

Inner circular layer

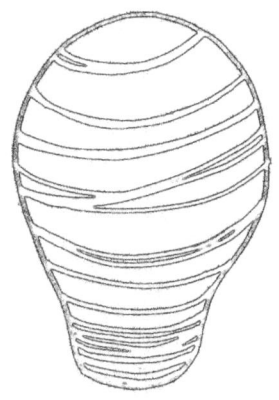

This layer of muscle runs around your body like a series of belts. The fibers are thickest just above the cervix, the opening at the bottom of the uterus and at the top of the uterus (the fundus) there is more space between the muscle fibers. With each surge during the first stage of labour the inner layer is drawn up and begins to bunch up at the top of the uterus. Because the fibers are relatively close together at the bottom, the first part of the first stage of labour is relatively easy. There is less effort involved in the first series of surges, which open the cervix the first 1-4cm. Once you get passed the 4cm mark and closer to 6cm dilated you will be experiencing 'established' labour and the surges will become more intense, you will be much less, if at all, interested in anything other than birthing. At this stage, the inner layer of uterine muscle is beginning to become quite bunched up at the top of the uterus and the outer layer of muscle has to work quite hard to achieve more opening with each surge.

Your Uterus During Birth

So, you might be starting to get a sense of what is happening and why it all seems to be such hard work. Just like running a marathon or moving house, during labour you are repeatedly using the same muscle group over and over for an extended period of time. Once the cervix has reached around 7-8cms open, your body will have been working hard for a while and the muscles will be subject to fatigue, you will also be experiencing more intense surges because the muscle fibers have to work harder to stretch the cervix open those final couple of centimeters.

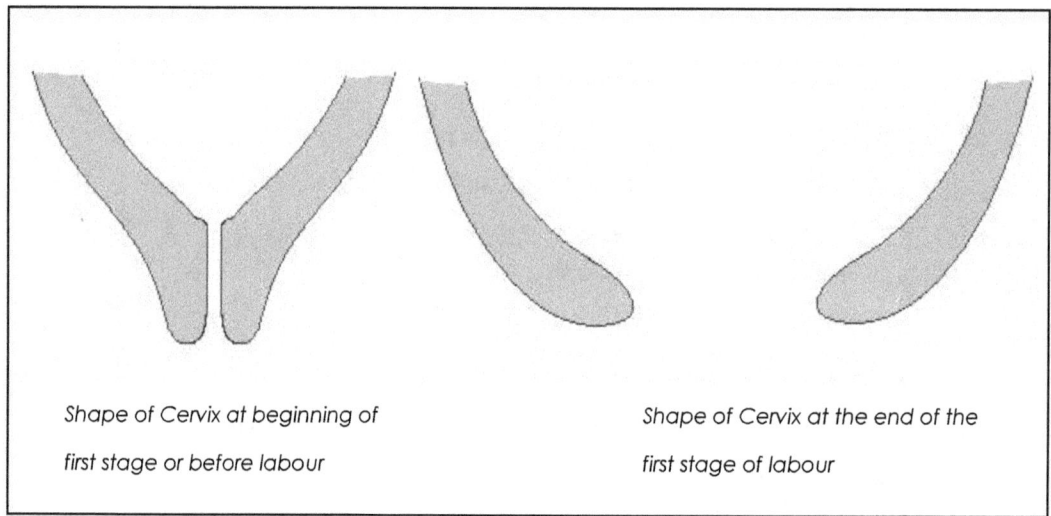

Shape of Cervix at beginning of first stage or before labour

Shape of Cervix at the end of the first stage of labour

The cervix is shaped just like the end of a balloon during pregnancy to create the 'neck' of the uterus. Just prior to or during the very early part of labour the cervix begins to 'thin'. That is, the muscles of the uterus draw the cervix out and up, stretching it up and around your baby's head to create an opening for your baby to pass through.

Once the cervix has been drawn up almost fully and the opening to the uterus is around 8-10cm you reach *transition*. Transition is the part between the first and second stages of labour when the muscles change their movement, the release of hormones changes and you will begin to experience a change in the way the surges feel.

From here, the job of the uterine muscle in second stage is to nudge your baby down and out. There is often a feeling of relief associated with the change in the surges and there is usually a strong sense of wanting to work with your body to help the uterus in its 'down and out' movement. The uterus works from the top down in second stage, when the surges are strongest at the top of the uterus, the fundus (however your attention will most likely be towards the bottom), where the fibers have bunched up during first stage. As the muscle surges, it also flexes and works to push down against your baby's bottom, using any amniotic fluid trapped between the top of the uterus and your baby as leverage.

After your baby has been born there will be a few more surges, usually a lot less intense, which will enable your uterus to expel the placenta. You may also experience mild surges or cramping when breastfeeding as the nipple stimulation prompts your body to release oxytocin, which will help the uterus to contract back down to its normal, non-pregnant size.

Unique Properties of the Uterus

The uterus has a number of properties that influence labour and the muscle's effectiveness during birthing:

Tone: the pressure within the muscle when it is not in surge, just like the tone in any other muscle. The difference between the tone of the uterus and that of other muscles is that you can actively strengthen (and thus tone) other muscles such as the bicep or thigh muscle by lifting weights or exercising. However, because the uterus is a smooth muscle you can't consciously contract or tone it. Many midwives and some research findings suggest that drinking *red raspberry leaf tea* during pregnancy helps to increase the tone of the uterus. Check with your midwife as to how much raspberry leaf tea you should drink.

Contractility: the ability of the muscle fibers of the uterus to work (or contract) in response to the chemical messenger, oxytocin. During the first stage of labour the upper part of the uterus (the fundus) contracts (shortens) to pull the lower part upwards to open the cervix.

Retraction, the uterus is special in its ability to *retract*, that is, it can retain the shortening and thickening of the muscle that occurs during each contraction, keeping the inner fibers drawn up and creating the opening of the cervix. This means that the uterus can hold open the cervix, maintaining the increasing dilation. With each surge in the first stage of labour the cervix opens a little more, between surges it maintains this opening through retraction and achieves further opening with the next surge.

Fundal dominance: this refers to the spontaneous wave of movement moving downward through the uterus and bearing down on your baby. Even during the first stage where the primary objective for the uterus is to open the cervix, there is still pressure at the top of the uterus created from the working of the muscle. The pressure within the uterus is stronger at the top (the fundus) to help nudge your baby down and out. During second stage this fundal pressure increases and moves in a wave like motion down the fibers of the uterus to further encourage your baby's movement down and out.

If your membranes are still intact (i.e. your waters haven't broken) the pressure from your baby's head on your cervix will be evenly distributed by physics of the amniotic fluid inside the amniotic sac. On the other hand, your membranes may release if your body needs the extra pressure of the baby's head directly on the cervix or the wall of the vaginal passage to help you to bear down (your voluntary efforts to birth your baby). This sometimes has the effect though of increasing the intensity of the sensation created by the surge as the pressure on the cervix is then likely to be uneven, with more pressure on one part of the cervix than another, depending on the positioning of your baby and your chosen birthing position.

Rhythm: the inherent rhythm of the muscle in response to its physical (stretched) and biochemical (hormonal) environment. Your relaxation and breathing will help your uterus to establish a harmonious rhythm within it. Just like your mind and your body, each of the three layers of uterine muscle need to work together for efficient and comfortable movement.

WORKING WITH YOUR UTERUS DURING LABOUR

If you are able to get a sense of the movement of the uterus and perhaps even visualise the movement or a representation of it and at the same time understand where the sensation of the surges is coming from and why it grows in intensity, each surge will be much easier to manage and work with.

Remember:
You only have to work with one surge at a time, deal with each surge as an independent moment that will pass.

Learn how to breathe with your surges (techniques suggested in the next section).

Do not wait for the next surge to come – once you are in established labour it will come, use the time between surges for yourself, to relax, to catch your breathing, to change positions or to have a drink.

Breathe out long and well after each surge to release any build up of energy or tension, relax and conserve your energy between surges to avoid fatiguing unnecessarily.

Remember that the uterus is a smooth muscle, its movement is involuntary, this means that you cannot flex or contract your uterus at will. Therefore, there is little use in pushing aggressively between surges – relax, the next surge will come.

During a Surge:
Allow your arms and legs, hands and feet to go loose and limp, totally relaxed throughout each surge so they are not wasting resources (i.e. blood, energy and oxygen).

During first stage work with the movement of the muscle in the uterus by 'breathing up' during surges and visualising the cervix softening and opening upwards.

During first stage, as far as possible, your body should be free of any tension. This doesn't mean that you can't move around, just avoid any unnecessary build up, like clenched fists for example.

During second stage you might feel the urge to push or bear down, use your upper abdominal muscles to help the uterus gain leverage in its downward movements. At the same time releasing the pelvic floor completely, all energy, flow and movement in your body needs to be down and out.

During second stage work with the movement of the muscle in the uterus by 'breathing down' during surges, imagining the vaginal path softening and opening to allow your body to release and let go (some women find it useful to imagine they are breathing out of the vagina).

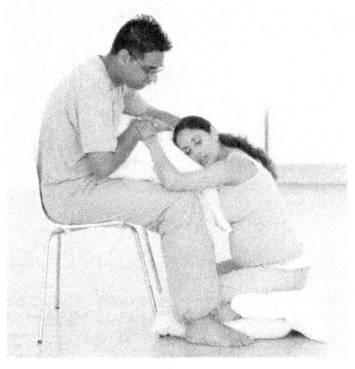

THE PROCESS – PART 2: HORMONAL ACTIVITY DURING LABOUR

Hormones are an integral part of the labour and birthing process. By using a few simple mind/body communication techniques such as relaxation, breathing techniques and affirmations, you can have a strong influence over the way your body releases and responds to the birthing hormones.

Four major groups of hormones are active during labour and birth:
- oxytocin, the hormone of love;
- endorphins, hormones of pleasure and transcendence;
- catecholamines, the hormones of excitement; and
- prolactin, the mothering hormone.

These hormones are common to all mammals and originate in our mammalian or middle brain, also known as the limbic system. For birth to proceed optimally, this part of the brain must take precedence over the neocortex, or rational brain (Buckley, 2002). This is just one of the reasons why using relaxation and hypnosis techniques during birth is so effective, hypnosis is a way of switching off the conscious mind and allowing the more primitive parts of the brain to work without criticism or hindrance from the thinking part of our brains.

Oxytocin

Probably, the most commonly talked about birth hormone is oxytocin, the hormone of love. This hormone is released by the brain during sexual activity, male and female orgasm, birth, and breastfeeding. As well as its other physiological jobs, oxytocin engenders feelings of love and altruism; as Michel Odent says, "Whatever the facet of Love we consider, oxytocin is involved (1999)".

Oxytocin is made in the hypothalamus, the "master gland" deep in our brains, and stored in the posterior pituitary, from where it is released in pulses. It is a crucial hormone in reproduction and mediates what have been called the ejection reflexes:
- the sperm ejection reflex with male orgasm (and the corresponding sperm introjection reflex with female orgasm);
- the fetal ejection reflex at birth (the powerful contractions at the end of labour, which birth the baby quickly and easily);
- the placental ejection reflex after the birth of the baby; and the milk ejection, or let-down reflex, in breastfeeding.

As well as reaching peak levels in each of these situations, oxytocin is secreted in large amounts in pregnancy, when it acts to enhance nutrient absorption, reduce stress, and conserve energy by making us sleepy.

Oxytocin is responsible for the rhythmic uterine surges of labour, and levels peak at birth through stimulation of stretch receptors in a woman's lower vagina as the baby descends. The high levels continue after birth, resulting in the birth of the placenta, and reduce the possibility of post-partum hemorrhage (this is why some doctors and midwives will offer an injection of synthetic oxytocin after the birth of your baby to help release the placenta).

Oxytocin release is also initiated by nipple stimulation (which can be used to help bring on labour if you are past your due date) and you may feel the less intense surges of the uterus during the first days of breastfeeding as the release of oxytocin helps the uterus return to its non-pregnant size.

Endorphins (beta-endorphin)

As a naturally occurring opiate, beta-endorphin has properties similar to pethidine, morphine, and heroin, and has been shown to work on the same receptors of the brain. Endorphins work by filling up and blocking the pain receptor sites in our brains so that pain messages can't get through to be perceived, interpreted or acted upon. Beta-endorphin is released under conditions of duress and pain, when it acts as an anesthetic.

Like the addictive opiates, beta-endorphin induces feelings of pleasure, euphoria, and dependency or, with a partner, mutual dependency (Buckley, 2002). Beta-endorphin levels are high in pregnancy and increase throughout labour as your uterine muscles work, just as they do for an elite athlete during a training session. The high levels help the labouring woman to alter her perception of pain and enter the deep level of relaxation that characterises a calm and comfortable birth.

Endorphins also stimulate the secretion of prolactin, the relaxing and "mothering" hormone that regulates milk production and gives you a psychological boost toward enjoyment of mothering. Laughter, massage and other pleasant physical stimulation encourage the release of endorphins during labour.

Catecholamines

The hormones epinephrine and norepinephrine (adrenaline and noradrenaline) are also known as the fight-or-flight hormones or, collectively, as catecholamines (CAs). They are secreted from the adrenal gland, above the kidney, in response to perceived threats, when they are responsible for activating the sympathetic nervous system for fight or flight.

As discussed in the section on the fight or flight response, activation of the sympathetic nervous system in this way is not helpful during labour. However, the hormones are complex and are actually needed for parts of labour to be efficient.

In the first stage of labour, high CA levels inhibit oxytocin production, therefore slowing or inhibiting labour. CAs also act to reduce blood flow to the uterus and placenta, and therefore to the baby. High levels of CAs have been associated with longer labour and adverse fetal heart rate patterns (Buckley, 2002).

During a calm labour however, when the moment of birth is imminent, these hormones act in a different way. There is a sudden increase in CA levels, especially noradrenalin, which activates the fetal ejection reflex. You will experience a sudden rush of energy; be upright and alert, with a dry mouth and perhaps the urge to grasp something. You may want to express sudden emotion, and the CA rush will cause several very strong contractions, which will have the effect of birthing your baby quickly and easily.

After the birth, CA levels drop steeply, you may feel shaky or cold as a consequence. A warm atmosphere is important, as ongoing high CA levels will inhibit oxytocin and therefore increase the risk of postpartum hemorrhage.

High CA levels at birth ensure that your baby is wide-eyed and alert at first contact with you and your partner. Your baby's CA levels also drop rapidly after a calm birth, being soothed by your contact.

Prolactin

Known as the mothering hormone, prolactin is the major hormone of breast milk synthesis and breastfeeding. Traditionally it has been thought to produce aggressively protective behaviour (the "lioness" effect or as some affectionately call it 'neurotic mother syndrome'!) in lactating females. Levels of prolactin increase in pregnancy, although milk production is inhibited hormonally until the placenta is delivered. Levels further increase in labour and peak at birth so that your body is ready for breastfeeding.

Prolactin is released in all healthy people during sleep, helping to maintain reproductive organs and immune function. In the mother, prolactin is released in response to suckling, promoting milk production as well as maternal behaviours (Buckley, 2002).

WORKING WITH YOUR HORMONES DURING LABOUR

As you can see, the hormonal involvement in pregnancy, labour, birthing and breastfeeding is complex, and not entirely understood by the research or medical communities. However, there are a few basics that we know for sure and, as individuals, can have some control over.

Oxytocin

Is needed to get the uterus working, so if you have gone past your due date and are wanting to bring labour on, you can try some things at home to encourage your body to release oxytocin – love making should be first on the list! A good female orgasm is one of the best ways to get the oxytocin flowing, use nipple and clitoral stimulation as well, which also encourage oxytocin release, to ensure you have covered all bases!

Sometimes during labour things seem to pause or even stop, if this occurs and you want to avoid artificial induction (use of the synthetic oxytocin) try nipple stimulation first (jump in the shower or ask the midwives for some privacy for a while). Any loving touch from your partner can also help (kisses, massage etc).

Beta-Endorphin

The number one way of ensuring that your endorphins will flow is to avoid the use of any medical pain relief. The body releases endorphins in response to hard work and discomfort, the introduction of an external agent precludes the perception of these stimuli and thus inhibits the release of your own natural pain relief. If you are able to go deep into relaxation and work with your body, you might find that very quickly you start to feel really (*really*) good – some women experience a warm tingling sensation as the *endorphin rush* releases and flows down through their bodies (this might be accompanied by a dopey, kind of drugged feeling – a lovely side effect of the oxytocin and endorphins working together).

You can also encourage the release of endorphins by eating spicy foods (maybe try this at home before you go to the hospital...), laughing and anything that leads to euphoria (try the *Light Touch Massage*)

Allow your body to do a bit of hard work (just like during exercise) and the endorphins will release in response.

Catecholamines (CA)

Good preparation, relaxation and calming techniques will help you to avoid the release of any stress hormones during the first stage of labour, when they are not needed. If you feel yourself becoming excited at the onset of labour (which is understandable!) try to do it in a very relaxed way...that is, avoid the build up of tension in your body in response to the excitement (positive stress has a similar effect on the sympathetic nervous system as negative stress). Take a bath or shower, go for a walk or ask your partner to help you with relaxation or massage.

Following a calm and undisturbed first stage of labour your body will naturally release just enough of the catecholamines (noradrenalin) to help your body release the energy needed for the final few surges, which will birth your baby. Use this energy. You will feel the build up of energy as the surge comes on, harness it with your breath in the lower part of your lungs and use it to create movement in your body - down and out.

The following chart represents the ideal flow of hormones throughout the birthing process. The practice effects of relaxation during pregnancy will decrease the release of catecholamines leading up to labour. Going into labour with a very low level of catecholamines will allow the oxytocin and beta-endorphin to flow freely, building up levels during the first stage of labour and peaking as your baby is born.

You will also notice the sudden rise and fall of catecholamines which provide your body with the energy it needs to bear down and birth your baby with those final few surges of second stage.

Awareness of how your uterus and hormones function during labour will help you to develop **Trust** in your body;

Your body knows what to do and what is right for you and your baby.

#1 Checking In – Self-Awareness Exercise

Thinking about labour and birthing, on a scale from 0 to 100, where 0 represents not at all and 100 means completely, how would you rate yourself right now in terms of:

0   100
_____

CONFIDENCE

0   100
_____

CALMNESS

Place a mark on the lines above to indicate how you feel right now Thinking about labour and birthing, on a scale from 0 to 100, where 0 represents not at all and 100 means completely, how would you want to feel during labour and birthing in terms of:

0   100
_____
CONFIDENCE

0   100
_____

CALMNESS

Place a mark on the lines above to indicate how you want to feel during labour and birthing

Has there been any change since you last rated yourself?

CHAPTER 2 TRUST

Most women seem to find that once they are aware of what is or will be, happening to their body during labour they feel much more at ease about the process. This knowledge or awareness removes the fear of the unknown to a large degree.

By this stage you have most probably also become aware of some of the sources of information about birthing you have relied on in the past. Movies, other people's traumatic stories, and even well meaning health care professionals wanting to 'prepare' you for the worst. However, rather than preparing you, these stories and negative depictions of birthing simply work to further instill fear and anxiety. Once you become aware that these are other people's stories and experiences and not your own you can move on towards preparing for a positive birthing experience. By making different choices during pregnancy and educating yourself about your body and your choices for birthing you are taking control of creating your own positive birthing story.

Once you are no longer fearful of labour you have the emotional space to develop a sense of trust in the process:

Trust that you know what is right for you and your baby;

Trust that nature and your body know how to birth your baby; and

Trust that your chosen birthing partner will nurture, support and protect you through labour and birthing.

DEVELOPING TRUST THROUGH FOCUS

When you are in a focused state of awareness and when you are birthing your baby, your mind becomes a powerful tool. You will focus on bringing your baby into the world and how the uterine muscles work, you will visualize the muscles drawing up and open.

The mind interprets messages from your body and it is this interpretation that creates sensations in your body. The body is essentially a robot. Thoughts and beliefs are powerful and if you believe that birth can be natural, calm and comfortable, then you are very much on the way to birthing your baby naturally. However, if you retain the beliefs that you have picked up over the years, those that suggest that childbirth is an unpleasant and medically controlled experience, then there is no place for your body to go but to follow these thoughts into fear, tension and pain.

Focus...

During pregnancy: **on health and wellbeing, on your preparations for your welcoming birthing, on finding evidence and support for your belief that birthing your baby is a positive experience.**

During labour: **on your breathing and physical relaxation, on the affirmations that support your beliefs, on your trust in your body and the process of birth, on the sensation of massage or water on your skin, on opening, releasing and letting go.**

There are many, many good people working in the field of childbirth who are working hard to ensure that as many mothers as possible walk out of their birthing rooms with pride and joy, with strength and confidence and a sense of achievement and satisfaction. It has given me such strength and encouragement to hear the birthing stories of mothers who I have worked with. Some who even birthed their babies at home without a doctor or midwife because their labours were going so calmly and smoothly they didn't feel the need to call anyone until it was too late for them to arrive on time! No pain, no drama and no pushing or yelling. Calm, welcoming birth can be yours if you believe that there is no need for it to be a frightening or unpleasant experience. If you believe you have the strength and power deep within you to take control of your body and your birthing. If you believe that babies should be welcomed into the world rather than 'delivered', focus on this during your pregnancy and birthing preparations and it will be so.

Choose to focus on the positive aspects of birthing, to take notice of women with positive birthing stories and to be supported by someone who also believes that birthing can be calm and welcoming.

Focus on the strength and coordination of your surges to maximise their effectiveness. If you are relaxed and understand how your body works, you are free to allow your uterus and birth path to relax and open, making birthing so much easier and much more comfortable.

TRUST AND HYPNOSIS/DEEP RELAXATION

I suggest the use of hypnosis, not as a method of birthing, but as a tool or technique that can be used to help you work with your body.

There are a number of ways you can use hypnosis, however, I will suggest that it be used primarily as a way of achieving deep relaxation, and with regard to some of the techniques, it is possibly even a little misleading to refer to them as hypnosis. However, some hypnotic techniques are discussed so it is useful to first understand what hypnosis is and is not.

Hypnosis for some people conjures up many images. The Stage Show, "Vatch da Vatch" or run around like a chicken. You would be surprised how many people come with this preconception asking, "when do you make us act like a chicken?".

To Milton Erickson, a highly skilled and world famous hypnotherapist, hypnosis is the way two people respond to each other, nothing more or less (Haley, 1986). There is not necessarily the need for a deep trance or a formal initiation such as counting backwards or swinging a watch. Hypnosis is simply a form of communication that, when used in hypnotherapy, allows one person to suggest to the other that they may wish to correct or change the way they think and behave. A person acting under hypnosis is not under anyone else's control and will not change or do anything if they do not wish to.

The reality of hypnosis is that you will always be in control,
you will always be in the driver's seat.

The most wonderful thing about hypnosis is that it is easy; almost anyone who wants to can achieve and be helped by hypnosis.

Hypnosis for pregnancy and childbirth can be used in a number of different ways:

- as therapy (hypnotherapy) for dealing with fear and anxiety;
- as a method for training the mind to shut off or ignore pain sensations;
- as a method for achieving deep relaxation;
- to help the new parents be accepting of the changes in their lives.

How effective is hypnosis for childbirth? As mentioned previously, using the techniques described here does not guarantee you a pain-free birth, but it will put you in an excellent position to work with your body and have a positive birthing experience. With adequate preparation and trust in the natural process of birth, most women can have much more relaxed and comfortable births, with many actually free of pain. Using hypnosis for childbirth is not an 'all or nothing' path, the outcome will depend on what you would like to use the hypnosis for and how much you practice the techniques suggested.

Benefits of using hypnosis for childbirth (Tuschhoff, 2003):

- Fewer drugs or no drugs at all means less risk of side effects on mother and baby.
- Shorter labours - resistance of the birthing muscles as a response to pain is minimised or eliminated.
- Time distortion through deep relaxation means that labour seems shorter.

- Brain activity shifts from the stress-prone right frontal cortex to the calmer left frontal cortex. This mental shift decreases the negative effects of stress and anxiety. There is also less activity in the amygdala, where the brain processes fear.
- An awake, energized mother, due to total relaxation throughout the birthing process.
- A calm, peaceful and welcoming birthing environment.
- Breech and posterior babies can be turned using hypnosis.
- Fewer interventions and complications during labour.
- Babies who are better sleepers and feeders due to fewer drugs in their systems and more feel good hormones they get from Mum.

Hypnosis also has many wonderful benefits during pregnancy and can be used to help with nausea, fatigue, leg cramps and heartburn as well as the physical and emotional benefits of deep relaxation for both mother and baby (Streeter, 2004). Use the CDs that came with this manual and also teach your partner how to help you into deep relaxation using the scripts provided.

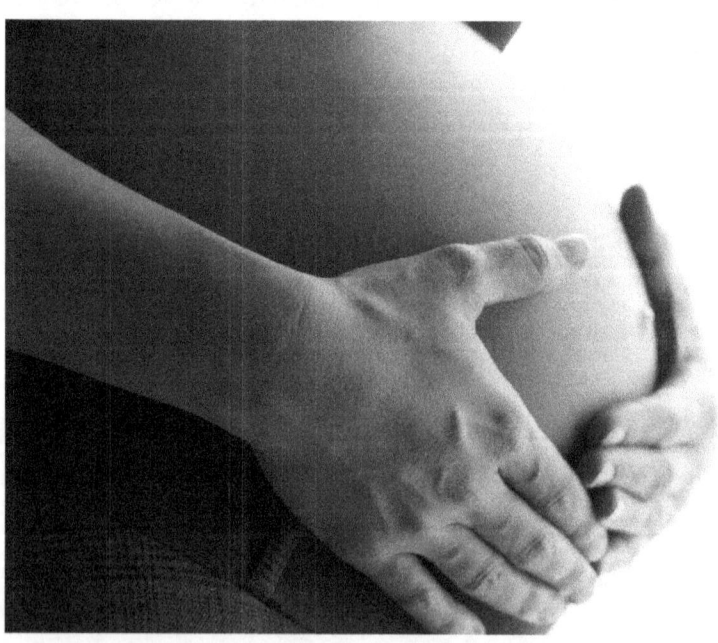

It is important to note that hypnosis alone will not 'deliver' the ideal birth. When placed in the right context of education about the human body, health and wellbeing and the process of natural labour, hypnosis can be a powerful tool for achieving the calm and empowered state of mind vital to a positive birthing experience.

> *The focused state of attention during your birthing puts you in control. A hypnotherapist's role, either in person or on CD, is to show you where the control panel is, deep inside, and how to use it. These techniques work just as well for first, second, third and even fourth time Mums, each are able to set aside any fears or negative thoughts they held about birthing and birth their baby very calmly and comfortably. This is because they have been taught how to go into the place where their beliefs and memories are stored and correct those thoughts that create fear and tension, deep within their minds, they have accepted the belief that childbirth is a natural process and a positive experience.*

Hypnotherapists stimulate your imagination and your inner mind through guidance and suggestions but at all times you retain complete selectivity over what is said, that is, you only accept what you choose to accept.

Hypnosis is simply the narrowing of the focus of attention. We all enter into hypnotic states constantly and we're not even aware of it:
Do you ever daydream?
Or become so engrossed in a book or movie that you forget your surroundings?
You might be driving along and then suddenly wonder how you got to where you are?

These are all states of self-hypnosis, in birthing you want to be focused on bringing your baby into the world, let all peripheral stimuli and foci go and concentrate on birthing.

Hypnosis allows you to bypass the essential but limited part of your mind, the conscious, analytical, and critical part and allows you to go deep into the part of the mind where your knowledge is stored. Once you are deep within your sub-conscious mind you are then able to re-organise your thoughts and beliefs and delete any negative or prohibiting thoughts to prepare for the calm and welcoming birth of your baby.

Only the mind can think. What the mind thinks the body creates. The body creates a physiological response to the thoughts that pass through the mind. When you think about it in the terms of the fight or flight response: the mind interprets an event as frightening and the body responds by quickening the heartbeat and rate of breathing. If you think of your favourite food, your mouth may begin to salivate, if you think of a person, perhaps a model or movie star that you might find sexually attractive, your body may also respond. We can use this mind/body link to our advantage during birthing.

If you are thinking and focusing on relaxation, on calming thoughts, or using visualisations that help you to work with the birthing process then your body will respond to these thoughts by also remaining calm, free of physical tension and focused on birthing your baby.

If your mind and body are calm your baby is also more likely to remain calm. If you are fearful or anxious in your mind during labour your body goes into 'fight or flight' mode and you are now aware of what can happen from there.

Remaining calm and relaxed throughout labour enables your uterus to function as effectively as possible making labour safer and more comfortable for you and your baby, possibly shortening the duration of the process and making it altogether a more positive experience.

<u>Hypnosis should not be the only tool you take into labour with you</u>, learn the breathing techniques, practice physical relaxation, ask your partner to learn the massage techniques and undertake preparation with regard to a birthing plan or birthing preferences.

Research suggests that 20 minutes of deep relaxation, through hypnosis or meditation has the same physiological benefits as 3 hours of sleep! (Dillbeck & Orme-Johnson, 1987)

If you are able to achieve 5-10minutes of deep relaxation between surges early on in your labour you will be energised and ready for second stage and bonding with your baby. This will be especially important if your labour happens during the night when you would normally be asleep.

From preparation and practice will come calmness and confidence.

USING HYPNOSIS FOR THE MANAGEMENT OF PAIN

Hypnosis or hypnotherapy should not be the only tool you use to prepare for labour and birth, nor should it be the only tool you take in with you to labour.

As well as the direct benefits of using hypnotherapy during pregnancy to help you prepare for a calm, confident birthing, there are other things that you and your partner can do to help ensure you get the most from you hypnotherapy or self-hypnosis sessions:

Releasing your fears. As you well know, there is a connection between fear and pain. Using hypnosis during pregnancy to release any fears you may become aware of (and even those you don't) will help you to look forward to the birth of your baby and ensure you are in the best possible emotional position for a calm and more comfortable birthing experience. Use the 'fear release' script on your **CD** to help with this process – the track is titled *Empowered Journey*.

Address your fears. What specifically, if anything, do you fear about birth? Maybe you don't call it fear but you need to identify things that bother you about birthing, or perhaps parenting. The concerns that most need addressing are those that might lead you to 'hold on' during labour. Educate yourself about your choices and choose not to dwell on things you cannot change or control. Again, use the 'fear release' script on your **CD** and talk to your partner about anything that is bothering, together you can come up with a plan for dealing with the issue should it arise.

Be informed. The more you know, the less there is to be afraid of. Going into labour for the first time, most of us are simply afraid of the unknown, the more you know and understand about how your body will work during labour the more empowered and in control you will feel. As well as reading and attending classes, use your own self-hypnosis or meditation to mentally and emotionally walk yourself through your birthing a few times in the weeks leading up to your due date. This way you can picture yourself in helpful labouring positions, see your partner being nurturing and supportive and see yourself feeling calm and relaxed. Having practiced this a few times you will almost feel as if you have already done it – just like an actor after the final dress rehearsal!

Choose a fearless birth partner. Remember, hypnosis is simply a form of communication. If you have a birth partner who is tense and fearful they will communicate this to you, either overtly in what they say or covertly through body language or choices they encourage. Fear is contagious. Bring your partner with you to your birth preparation classes or share with them the important parts of this book to ensure they know their role and what to expect on the day.

Take responsibility for your birth choices and decisions. Using hypnosis or deep relaxation during your pregnancy will contribute to an overall feeling of calmness and confidence, which you will carry with you into labour and the birthing suite. When you are calm and confident you are in control, of your body and your birthing, and you will have put in place measures for ensuring your most important birthing preferences are respected, regardless of any special circumstances.

Be selective in choosing your healthcare provider. Does your doctor or midwife reinforce your trust in your body and your ability to give birth? You also need to trust this person, trust that they will understand and respect your birthing choices and work with you completely in any special circumstance. You might also like to talk to your doctor or midwife about the use of hypnosis or other relaxation techniques for birthing – do your beliefs match theirs? If not, ask yourself if this person can still provide the service you want from them – possibly or maybe you would like to find someone else?

Understand labour and the birth process. Self-hypnosis creates a focused state of awareness, if you are aware of and understand how your uterus is working during labour you can focus on the positive aspects of the sensations and the process.

Working with the medical aspects (such as blood pressure and electronic fetal monitoring). During your hypnosis or relaxation practice, build in some distractions. Think about what equipment is likely to be used during your labour and ask your partner to come in and, in a very symbolic or representative way, pretend to take your blood pressure or monitor your baby's heartbeat while you practice remaining deeply relaxed.

Be aware of the options available for medical pain relief, such as the gas and epidural anesthesia. There is no medal for suffering needlessly during labour or birth. DO NOT ALLOW YOURSELF TO SUFFER – it is so much braver to ask for help than to suffer in silence. There is no failure in accepting that this is bigger than you expected and you need help to manage the process so that you can get back to focusing on welcoming your baby. You can still employ the relaxation and calming techniques in conjunction with other forms of pain relief.

Learn to release and let go. The more you practice the relaxation and breathing techniques the easier they will come to you on the day. Use self-hypnosis to help you to take on the belief that your body knows what to do, all you have to do is relax fully and allow each surge to work.

Learn to relax your body totally and completely. Physical relaxation is essential for a more comfortable birthing experience. It helps manage discomfort around the uterus, minimises the use of oxygen and other essential resources by other parts of the body and ensures that you do not tire or fatigue prematurely. Use the **CD** to help you learn to do this, the *Gentle Surge* relaxation track on the CD is designed to help you achieve deep physical relaxation. Once you have practiced with these for a while and feel comfortable with the level of relaxation you are able to achieve move on and try the *Rapid Relaxation* Technique outlined in the techniques section.

THE PROCESS OF SELF-HYPNOSIS

Self-hypnosis is simply the process of taking yourself into the relaxed state of body and mind where you are free to focus your thoughts on images, concepts or affirmations that will be useful to you for labour, birth or parenting (or anything else that you choose to use it for!).

It is useful to be able to do this yourself for a number of reasons; however, it is not essential. You have the CD to work with and the 'scripts' for your partner to use with you. Some women find it empowering to be able to take themselves into a deeply relaxed state and not be reliant on anyone or anything else, or you might find that a CD player or willing partner are not always easy to come by! It also helps to enhance your guided relaxation or hypnotherapy experience if you are practiced in self-hypnosis as well.

You will notice on the **CD** that there is a pattern in the way the relaxation sessions are put together.

You also have a number of 'scripts' in this workbook to help guide you as to the type of thing you might think about when you are taking yourself into self-hypnosis.

Remember, there is nothing magic to hypnosis. Anyone who wants to can achieve a state of self-hypnosis, a state of focused awareness where you allow your body to relax while you mind concentrates on something that is going to help you achieve your goal/s.

Follow these simple steps to practice and achieve self-hypnosis:

Eye closure – a seemingly obvious first step (after finding a comfortable place to sit or lie), however it is an important step. Most people are able to relax and focus more clearly with their eyes closed and find that it is as simple a choosing to allow your eyes to gently close. Other people find it effective to stare upwards at the ceiling or a light fixture for a while, until they feel their eyes starting to want to close, resist for a few moments and then let your heavy eyelids roll down.

Physical Relaxation – something to try with the CD or with a partner first perhaps, or you might already be experienced in physical relaxation from yoga classes. You might use the *Rapid Relaxation* or *Progressive Relaxation*, just going through these in your own mind, using the *relaxation breath* to allow the relaxation to flow down through your body. You will find information on each of these techniques further along in the workbook in the *Work* Chapter.

Deepening – simply the process of allowing your mind to relax. Some people find it helpful to count backwards from 10 down to 1 or to imagine they are walking down a flight of stairs or down a long hallway. You could imagine walking along a beach with your feet sinking softly into the sand or along a track, deep into a beautiful rainforest. Whatever the image or concept you use, the idea is that you are going on a journey, deeper into relaxation and deeper into your mind. Many people find it comforting to imagine they are travelling to a 'safe place', a place where no one can disturb them, where no one can know what they are thinking about and where they are in complete control of their mind and body.

Focused Awareness – this is the part of the process where the 'hypnotherapy', or meditation, takes place. Once you have reached your destination or 'safe place' you can then focus your awareness on an affirmation, image or concept that will be useful to you in achieving your goal. Most people find it useful to have decided what they are going to focus on before going into self-hypnosis. There are affirmations provided in this workbook, or you can make up your own. There is also a section on the use of visualisation and imagery, which might give you some ideas about what to focus on. Or you might like to imagine going deep inside your body where you can sneak a peak at your baby's face and think about a conversation you would like to have with your baby, telling her or him how loved they are and how much you are looking forward to holding them in your arms – a wonderful bonding experience.

Waking – when you are ready, it is very important to bring yourself back up out of self-hypnosis very slowly. During this deeply relaxed state you will experience physiological changes, including a slowing of your heartbeat, slowing of your breathing rate and a change in your brainwave activity. If you suddenly just open your eyes or sit up etc., your body will experience some shock at having been jerked out of the deeply relaxed state into alertness. Bring yourself up slowly by counting from 1 up to 10, by letting your awareness shift gradually from processes within your mind and body to the outside world (e.g. feeling of the bed beneath you, sounds around you etc). And when you are ready, open your eyes.

For most people starting out with self-hypnosis, the process may take 10-15 minutes, but with only a little practice you might find that you will surprise yourself at how much time has passed during your relaxation session – a nice 'side-effect' during labour!

Can women really give birth without experiencing pain? Yes, however there are many variables in labour and birth that can affect the outcome, and couples need to have a positive but realistic view of hypnosis for childbirth. Each pregnant woman and her partner need to feel empowered about the choices they have during labour and how they might interact with their caregivers to achieve the best outcome for mother and baby. Many a wonderful birth has been thwarted by not realizing how to make positive, informed choices (Dick-Read, 2004). Choosing to incorporate hypnosis in your birthing toolbox will help you focus your energy and awareness towards a positive birthing outcome.

A great deal of research supports the view that maternal anxiety is directly related to physical and emotional difficulty during birthing (Pratt, Wood & Alman, 1988). Without a doubt, women using hypnosis are much calmer and more relaxed during labour, which automatically creates more comfort, as well as having 'powerful' post-hypnotic suggestions to actually reduce or eliminate pain and fear (The physical and biochemical basis for this effect is explained in the section on the 3 paths to reducing pain).

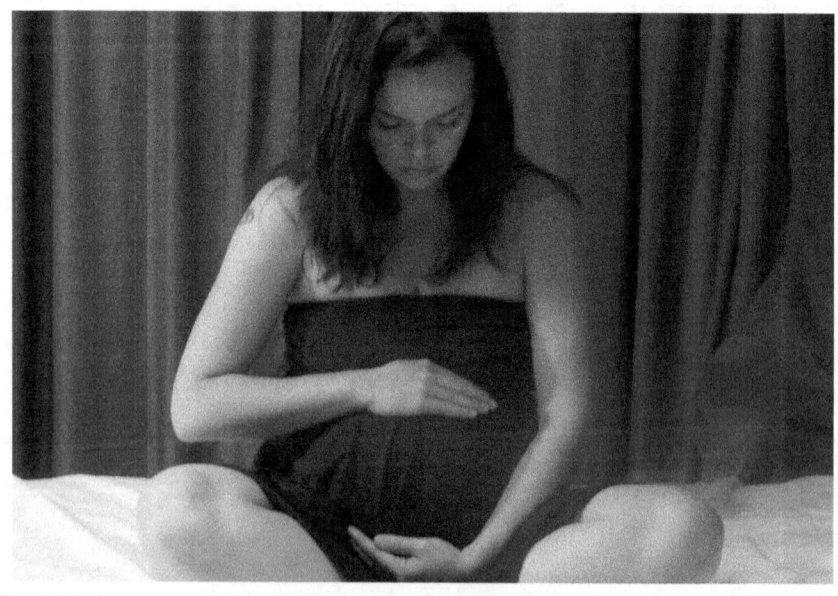

MANAGING PAIN DURING BIRTHING

Understanding The Cause Of Labour Pain

It takes a lot of pushing and stretching to move a baby the size of a melon through a cervical opening that starts out as the size of a kidney bean. Muscles don't flex or tissues stretch without letting your body know it. Contrary to popular belief, it's usually not the contracting uterine muscles that produce the discomfort. Like any other muscle in your body, uterine muscles don't hurt unless they are forced to work in a way they were not designed to. Yet when a muscle is overly tired, the natural chemistry and electrical activity within the muscle tissues get out of balance. These physiological changes produce pain.

Most of the discomfort during labour originates in the stretching of the cervix, vagina, and surrounding tissues as the baby passes through. During labour the uterine contractions work to pull the cervical muscle up out of the way so that the baby's head can then be pushed through. The muscles and ligaments in the pelvis are richly supplied with receptors in the nerves, so the stretching produces powerful sensations that have the potential to be interpreted as pain, especially if there is tension in the surrounding muscles.

In order to manage any discomfort during labour well you need to understand how your body processes pain and how your mind perceives it:

- As a surge begins, tissues stretch, and the tiny pressure receptors in the nerves are stimulated, sending lightning-fast impulses along the nerves to the spinal cord.

- In the spinal cord these impulses must pass through a system that works like a gate that can stop some impulses and allow others to pass through into the brain.

Once a sensory message reaches the brain there is the potential to interpret the message and respond or react accordingly.

> The **Gate Control Theory of Pain** was first proposed in 1965 by psychologist Ronald Melzack and anatomist Patrick Wall. They suggested that there is a "gating system" in the central nervous system that opens and closes to let pain messages through to the brain or to block them.
>
> According to the gate control theory of pain, our thoughts, beliefs, and emotions may affect how much pain we feel from a given physical sensation. The fundamental basis for this theory is the belief that psychological as well as physical factors guide the brain's interpretation of painful sensations and the subsequent response. Many athletes do not experience pain during the intense activity of the game. After the game, when they turn their attention to their injuries, the pain suddenly appears to come from nowhere. Many pain sufferers find that their pain is worst when they feel depressed and hopeless - feelings that may open the pain gate- however, they also notice that the pain is not so bothersome when they are focused on doing something that demands attention or is enjoyable. Although the physical cause of pain may be identical, the perception of pain is dramatically different.

The perception of pain can be influenced at three sites:

1. **Where it's produced in the first place (i.e. the uterus),**
2. **At the 'gate' in the brain stem (at the top of the spinal cord in the base of the skull), and**
3. **In the brain where the pain is perceived (in your mind).**

In deciding which birthing tools might work best for you, ensure that you practice techniques that address the management of pain at all <u>three</u> of these sites. Have two or three techniques for each to allow you to try different things.

To manage discomfort around the uterus – creating a good working environment for the uterus:

These techniques will help you to minimise the number of pain messages created. The main techniques that will help you to create a good working environment for your uterus are:

The breathing techniques - Breathe, don't hold your breath or let your breath 'get away' from you during labour. The working muscles of your uterus and your baby both need oxygen for wellbeing.

Physical relaxation - Relax your body fully and completely to avoid placing unnecessary external pressure on the uterus as it is working. Use your relaxation techniques to keep your muscles from getting tired and tense and avoid unnecessary fatigue. Relaxation will also help you to avoid wasting precious energy and oxygen in tense muscles that aren't needed for birthing.

Good body positioning throughout labour - Use efficient positions for labour that keep your muscles working in the way they were designed to without fatiguing unnecessarily. Think about the movement of your baby through your body, past the bony pelvis, navigating its way past your tailbone and out through the pelvic outlet, what positions might best help your baby on its journey?

To manage the working of the 'gate' – sensory stimulation for your central nervous system (CNS):

These techniques will help you to block any pain messages that are created, preventing them from reaching your brain. The main techniques that will help you to provide sensory stimulation to your CNS and thus help to 'close the gate' to unpleasant sensations are:

- **Massage (light touch or other labour massage techniques);**
- **Water (bath or shower);**
- **TENS machine;**
- **Environmental stimuli (e.g. music, essential oils, favourite photos, yummy snacks, stress ball or other object to squeeze or stroke).**

The idea is to close the gate in the spinal cord so pain messages can't get through. A pleasant touch stimulus, such as: the light touch, other massage, water (shower or bath) or the use of a TENS machine sends positive impulses that can actually block the transmission of pain impulses through the spinal cord. Messages from the sensations crated by these techniques also travel much faster through the spinal cord, reaching the brain before any pain messages have a chance to get through. This is why we tend to 'rub it better' when we knock or bump ourselves accidentally.

You can also cause gridlock at the gate by sending through a lot of competing stimuli, overwhelming the central nervous system with pleasant stimuli. The light touch massage and TENS machine are especially designed for this purpose and used in conjunction with music, essential oils, or other pleasant stimuli, can have a strong, overwhelming effect in blocking any pain messages passing through the CNS.

To manage the perception of sensory messages in the brain – top down management:

These techniques will help you to disregard or distract yourself form any messages about pain or discomfort that might have made their way through. The main techniques that will help you focus your awareness and prevent processing pain messages are:

- **Guided relaxation or self-hypnosis;**
- **Focus on your breath;**
- **Laughter or other endorphin producing activities;**
- **The use of imagery and visualisation;**
- **The use of affirmations during labour and birth;**
- **Focused awareness of the sensation of water or massage on your skin.**

You can fill up the receptor sites in the brain so that the pain-messages, despite making it to the brain, have no place to go (a bit like getting into the city on a busy day and not finding a place to park your car).

Blocking access to this third pain-perception site is how pain-relieving drugs work. You can achieve the same effect naturally by manufacturing your body's own natural painkillers, endorphins. Use self-hypnosis, massage, laughter, deep relaxation and water to help with this. In addition to the effect of the endorphins, you will also take up processing power with these techniques. We are very clever creatures but can only do so many things at once, if you are focusing on your breath, visualising the breath going down to your baby as your body opens up and moving gently through the bath water, all at the same time, there isn't much brain space left to perceive any messages about pain!

You can also choose to reinterpret the messages sent from the uterus. By understanding the workings of the uterus during birthing and focusing on welcoming your baby, you are able to experience the tightening and pressure of each surge as a positive sensation. Preparing yourself for labour, and being relatively free of fear and anxiety before going into labour will help you achieve this.

With <u>Awareness</u> and <u>Trust</u> you are now ready to <u>Work</u> with your body.

TERMINOLOGY FOR A CALM, CONFIDENT, WELCOMING BIRTH

The way we talk about birthing has an enormous impact on the way we think about birthing. Words commonly associated with birthing, such as 'contraction', have long standing connotations, of pain and of being out of control; these words are generally fear inducing for most women. Changing the words we use to talk about birthing will help women and their partners to acknowledge that this is a natural process . That their bodies have been 'designed' to do the job and they have within them natural resources that will help them manage and work with the process.

Suggested Term:	*Otherwise known as...*
Surge or wave	Contraction
Birthing Partner	Coach
Birthing	Delivery
Receive the baby	Catch or deliver the baby
Birthing or birthing process	Labour
Pressure or tightening	Pain
Membrane	Sac
Membranes release	Waters break
Breathing down	Pushing
Special circumstances	Complications
Seal or show	Mucous Plug
Thinning and opening	Effacing and dilating

"I would say that although the birth didn't go exactly to plan, we always felt as though we had plenty of time to make decisions and we used the relaxation countdown/meditation in the early stages and before the eventual c-section to relax. Stewart was extremely reassuring and seemed very confident to me. I also found that I reassured myself with the information about the contractions, telling myself the intensity was OK and the baby/my body was going through all the stages it needed to. So for the most part I was able to trust that my body knew what it was doing and mentally 'allow' the body it to what it needed to." Christina, mum to Nate 2008.

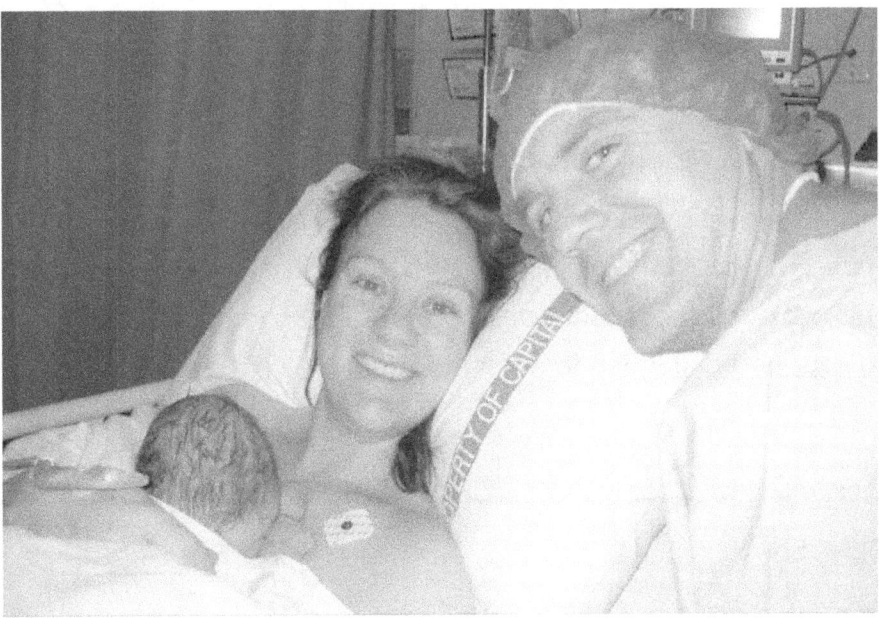

If you go into labour looking for pain…you will probably find it. Preparing for a calm and welcoming birth will help you manage the sensations of labour.

#2 Checking in – Self-Awareness Exercise.

Thinking about labour and birthing, on a scale from 0 to 100, where 0 represents not at all and 100 means completely, how would you rate yourself <u>right now</u> in terms of:

0   100

CONFIDENCE

0   100

CALMNESS

Place a mark on the lines above to indicate how you feel <u>right now</u>

Thinking about labour and birthing, on a scale from 0 to 100, where 0 represents not at all and 100 means completely, how would you <u>want to feel during labour and birthing</u> in terms of:

0   100

CONFIDENCE

0   100

CALMNESS

Place a mark on the lines above to indicate how you <u>want to feel during labour and birthing</u>

Has there been any change since you last rated yourself?

CHAPTER 3 WORK

This section is called **Work** for a reason – for most women, labour is hard work. Remember- hard work doesn't have to include pain, but it does require effort and preparation to do it well. A runner doesn't just turn up to the start of a 42km marathon without some preparation or training, and certainly doesn't get to the finish line without hard work – birthing well also requires preparation and work. Some of the following techniques are for training and preparation, others are for the work on the day, most are useful for both.

There are many techniques for enabling your mind and body to work together. Those presented here by no means represent an exhaustive list but one that has been shown through research and/or experience to be helpful and effective in creating a positive birthing experience.

As a general guide for your birth preparations:

- If nothing else, learn the skill of physical relaxation and plan for the use of a breathing technique of some sort, preferably those suggested here. It would also be great if you find ways of combining pre-natal bonding with your relaxation practice.

- Ensure you are aware of and understand the workings of the uterine muscles and how the fight or flight response hinders their effectiveness.

- Use the *Birthing Affirmations* on the CD or the copy provided in this workbook to help you reinforce your positive beliefs about birthing (add to this your ability and resolve to disregard other people's negative stories or advice).

- Practice the various self-hypnosis and relaxation techniques to take you even deeper into relaxation. Use the *Gentle Surge* track on the CD as well as the other techniques suggested.

- The next step is to prepare your birthing preferences and use the *Calming Fear Release* and *Connecting Mind & Body* tracks on the CD to complete your emotional preparation.

Work at it...
Practice develops skill and association – both of which will ensure you will slip easily into deep relaxation during labour.

BREATHING TECHNIQUES

The breathing techniques are a very important part of birthing calmly and comfortably. It is essential that you keep the oxygen flowing around your body and to your baby. You need to breathe in well to ensure you have enough oxygen for your body, your working uterus and your baby. You need to breathe out well to expel carbon dioxide and waste products from the working muscle.

Candice Pert, who discovered endorphins and the other chemical messengers in our body, says in her book *The Molecules of Emotion*, that "Conscious, controlled breathing techniques employed by both the yogi and the woman in labour are extremely powerful". There is a wealth of data showing the quantity and kind of peptides that are released from the brain stem when controlled breathing is practiced, (peptides is another word for hormones) and since many of these peptides are endorphins, the body's natural chemicals for relieving discomfort and pain, you soon achieve a calm comfortable state within your body (and relief from any discomfort you may feel). So it's no wonder that many modalities, both ancient and contemporary, have discovered the power of this focused, controlled breathing.

Candice Pert goes on to say the peptide respiratory link is well documented. Virtually any peptide found naturally in the body can be found in the respiratory centre. This may provide the scientific rationale for the powerful healing effects of consciously focused and controlled breathing.

Herbert Benson, in his book *Timeless Healing* talks about a journey to the Himalayas where he went into a Zen Buddhist monastery during a snowstorm. The Buddhist monks came in with their clothes dripping wet and preceded to go into a meditative state and subsequently were able to raise their body temperature to 40 degrees. He was amazed by this experience and wrote that it reinforces the body as a robot theory; what the mind thinks the body will follow.

Practice the breathing techniques as often as you can during your pregnancy and especially during your relaxation times and times when you experience Braxton Hicks or other birthing type sensations.

> **There are three breathing techniques to learn:**
>
> ### 1. Relaxation Breathing
>
> *(for pregnancy, first stage of labour & after each surge)*
>
> ### 2. Controlled Breathing
>
> *(for during surges in the first stage of labour & transition)*
>
> ### 3. Breathing Down
>
> *(for during surges in the second stage of labour)*

Relaxation Breathing

Breathing is the essence of relaxation and a very important tool in keeping your body calm. The first breathing technique is *Relaxation Breathing*, it is designed to initiate relaxation and release tension from your body. **The basic idea is to breathe in to the sound of *re-* and out to the sound of *-lax*.**

As you inhale, breathe in all the *re* in, refresh, rejuvenate, re-energize, relax; and as you exhale, let go of any stress, tension or anxiety and release into loose, limp, and *lax*. If you like, imagine breathing in peace and relaxation and breathing out stress and tension.

Technique - First put one hand on your abdomen and the other on your chest, feel the rise of your chest as you breathe in. Imagine filling your lungs with oxygen under the lower hand on your abdomen so that you see your hand rising. As you exhale feel your chest caving in first. In to *re* - abdomen rising first followed by the chest... and out to *lax*— chest falling first followed by the abdomen. Some women prefer to count – in for a count of 4 and out for a count of 6-8 (whichever you can manage). The emphasis is on a long and complete exhalation (out breath) - just like a *sigh*, you might also find that it is helpful to make the *sigh* type sounds as you exhale during labour - "*ahhhh*". With practice it will soon come naturally and you will not need to think about technique.

Breathe this way every time you want to bring yourself into relaxation. It will become a trigger for your body to release any tension it may be holding. Practice – when you sit down at the end of your day, take about 3 or 4 of these relaxation-type breaths (always stop if you become light headed) and you will start to feel your body relax in response. And you will relax more and faster each time you practice.

Preparation - Practice this technique a few times each night before you fall off to sleep or each time to listen to a track on the **CD.**

You might also like to practice this technique if you experience any sort of emotional stress and need to regain your composure or want to avoid the stress hormones from reaching your baby. If you practice relaxation breathing at these times you will very quickly develop an association between this type of breathing and relaxation. Once the association is well developed the breath will be a trigger for your body to go deeply into relaxation without you needing to use any conscious thought or effort. The more you practice the stronger the association. The stronger the association the better the trigger will work during labour.

Work - During labour and birthing use the relaxation breathing each and every time you feel a surge release and let go. As you feel the pressure or tightening subside, take 2 or 3 of the relaxation breaths and release any tension that may have built during the surge. Use the breath to initiate or maintain deep rest and relaxation between surges, to conserve your energy for when it is needed.

Use the relaxation breathing to help you if your relaxation has been interrupted or if there has been a distraction.

Use this breath if you find things getting away from you a bit in the excitement of realising *this is it* or the intense part nearing transition. You need to make sure your partner knows the technique and can help you re-establish the pattern of breath if need be.

> *Partner* – *As well as prompting and encouraging the relaxation breathing after each and every surge and if you need to help reinitiate deep relaxation use the technique for yourself to help maintain a sense of calmness and wellbeing.*
>
> *Your emotional state will transfer to your partner so make sure you are sending calmness and confidence - love and support.*

Controlled Breathing

This method of breathing takes a bit of extra practice. It is the one you will use through your surges in your first stage of labour. The technique can be practiced when you feel a Braxton-Hicks surge; when you feel your uterus tightening, practicing for real labour.

Technique - The controlled breathing is much like the breath control you would use during hard exercise, a big in breath and a big out breath, with a steady controlled rhythm.

Someone standing right next to you should be able to hear your breath as it passes in and out – "ah(in)…phoooo(out)…ah(in)…phoooo(out)" – the sounds come from the air entering your throat on the in breath and passing your lips on the out breath. Alternately, the sounds might resemble the mantra *aum or om*, "auuuuuuu" (in)…. "mmmmmm" (out).

Preparation – *Practice this technique:*
- When you go for a walk, uphill or up a set of stairs.
- Swimming is a great way to practice a long, slow form of controlled breathing.
- During pregnancy, practice this breathing if you experience a cramp, stub your toe or experience any sort of physical discomfort.

Work - As you feel a surge coming on begin the breathing with big, deep rhythmical breaths. Keep control of the breaths and don't let your breathing 'get away from you'. Using this technique you might get a very real sense of working with the muscles of the uterus as they tighten and shorten. Remember to allow the rest of your body to relax.

The visualisation of blowing up balloons or your surge being similar to a wave of energy passing through you, breathing up one side and down the other, can be very helpful. The rest of your body beneath the wave is totally relaxed and still while you breathe up and over or through each surge. Thoughts and imagery can work wonders and can be easily used as prompts during labour by your partner along with encouraging your breathing.

> ***Birthing partner*** *- watch closely that the breathing is slow and rhythmic and that Mum does not hold her breath at any time. Her body and your baby are dependant on the oxygen from each breath.*

While breathing in, focus your attention on your rising abdomen the same as you did for the relaxation breathing and bring the surge up as much as you can. Visualize the wave of energy as it passes through your abdomen and your uterus, turning the energy into movement and using this to ease your baby out. Slowly exhale, breathing down and out. Give your breath to your baby, gently and slowly exhaling down into your vagina. Soft, gentle and comfortable.

Using your imagination you can think about the oxygen flowing through your body and the effect that it is having, a calm tranquillising effect on your system, as the oxygen combines with your red blood cells and flows down to your uterus and your baby. Use your imagination, your baby is dependent on your oxygen. Do not hold your breath, give it to your body and your baby.

The most important thing is to maintain the breathing for the entirety of each wave. The Controlled Breathing is a key to maintaining control

over your labour. The goal is to focus on your breath, using it to control other responses in your body, it is your gear-stick to labour.

Keep your body loose and limp at all times during your labour (remember – this doesn't mean you can't move around, just avoid any unnecessary build up of muscular tension).

Breathing Down

As your birth unfolds and you move towards the end of the first stage, you will be experiencing regular, rhythmic surges in your body. If you have any concerns or are feeling unsure about what is happening, ring the hospital, they are there to talk to you and help you- this is their job.

You will instinctively know when it is time to go to the hospital – your surges will take over your whole being. Birth will be the only thing your existence is about at that time – your whole purpose. Or you might just feel the need to be in the place where you will birth your baby – to feel settled and secure. When you are ready, make your way to the hospital or prepare yourself at home. Once in your birthing room you may like to have a bath, walk around or maybe even just lie on the bed and relax. Whatever you feel like doing is good. Women in labour know instinctively how to find their own comfortable position. At the end of the first stage you will know something is changing. You may have a fullness in the pelvic area, feeling that bulge and pressure as your baby moves down into the vaginal path. Your surges will begin to change in the way they feel.

Previously you will have been using the *Controlled Breathing Technique,* focusing on the breath in as equally as the breath out and visualising the inner circular muscles pulling up. The muscles are now ready to put all their energy behind your baby and are starting to nudge your baby down. You will most likely (but not necessarily) become aware of a strong urge to bear down or push.

The Breathing Down techniques requires just a few slight modifications to the controlled breathing so that you breathe down and help your uterus in its work. You can use this technique even if you are only 9cms dilated, because you're not pushing aggressively you are just maybe helping that last little bit of cervix to open.

Technique - *Take a deep breath in, pulling the energy of the breath deep down into your lungs or your belly.* Very slowly and gently exhale, allowing just a very light and gentle stream of air to escape from your partially open lips or from your nostrils (it may help to imagine a feather just in front of your lips and your breath creating only very slight movement of the feather) .

Holding the energy of your breath in your belly or upper abdomen, work with the breath almost as leverage to help your uterus nudge your baby down and out (during practice you may find it more useful to think of your bowels working the waste down and out).

Preparation - *The best time to practice this technique is on the toilet when you are using your bowels. Take a big breath in as you prepare to exert energy and create the movement down and out. Allow your breath to escape through your lips or nostrils as you work through the movement.*

Combine the breathing practice with relaxing your pelvic floor completely. We aren't in a position to do this very often but on the toilet is a safe place. Let your pelvic floor muscles release and focus on that part of your body opening out. During birthing a tight and toned pelvic floor can get in the way of an easy birth, while it is still important to practice your pelvic floor muscle exercises, you also need to know how to relax these muscles.

Hopefully you will get to practice this technique every day – you might even find that the technique helps to relieve your constipation!

Work - Take a quick but full and deep breath in as you feel the wave rising and the need to bear down takes over. Exhale in a very slow and controlled manner throughout the surge.
Imagine breathing down through your vaginal path, using your breath to show your baby the way out.

Do not try to make the exhalation last the length of the surge if it becomes uncomfortable, release and take another big but quick breath in and slowly exhale again. Take as many of these types of breath as you need to work with and maximise the effectiveness of each surge.

- Use your upper abdominal muscles to help push down.
- Focus on allowing your pelvic floor to relax and open out completely – release and let go.
- Once the surge has passed, take a few relaxation breaths, rest and wait for the next surge.

Many studies have shown that it is not good to push too aggressively. Old training tells the mother to hold her breath and push with all she can, hanging onto everything tightly and turning red in the face. This can break the small blood vessels in the eyes because of the pressure building up in and around the eyes and in some cases can cause quite a severe headache (and also hemorrhoids and damage to the vagina and birth canal). If the baby is being monitored you will see the baby's heartbeat drop as the mother violently pushes hanging onto each breath and depriving her body and her baby of oxygen.

Research shows that there is no difference in the length of the second stage whether you breathe your baby down or hold your breath and push. The only difference between these two techniques seems to be the risk of injury to yourself.

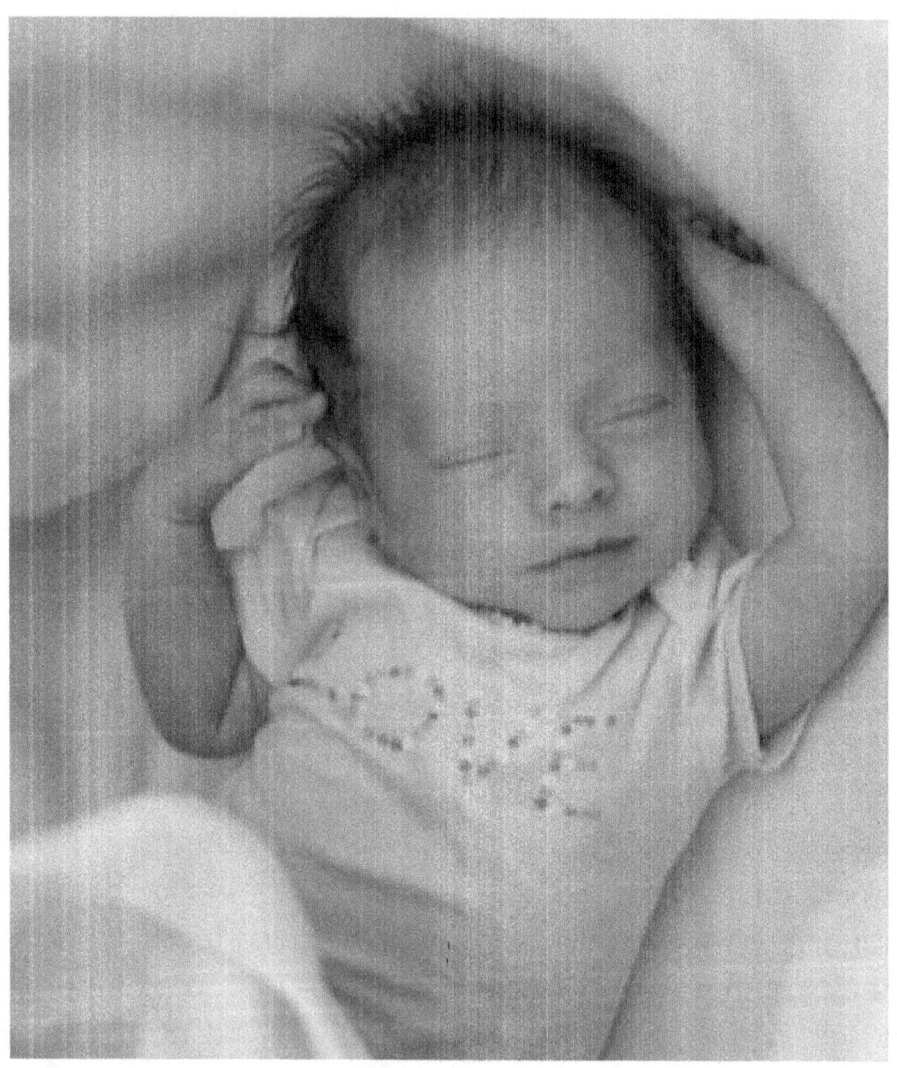

Summary – Breathing Techniques

RELAXATION BREATHING:

For **relaxation between surges** and to give more oxygen to your baby. A big deep sigh.

- If you want to use a prompt – breath in to the count of 4 and out to the count of 6 or breath in to the sound of *re-* out to *–lax*.
- **inhale**: imagine the stomach rising like a balloon - stomach first and then chest.
- **exhale**: chest releases & shoulders sink.
- As you exhale, release and let go of all tension.
- The in breath is slightly shorter than the out breath. The emphasis is on the out breath, relax *into* the breath out.
- Practice everyday as you prepare to relax or sleep.

CONTROL BREATHING:

Used **during waves** – start to control your breathing as soon as you feel the rise of the surge, maximising the oxygen you are taking in.

- your goal is to keep breathing in a deep and controlled manner. By working with the rise of the surge you help the vertical muscles draw up the lower inner circular fibers, opening the cervix. Just like the type of breath you use when jogging or walking up a steep hill or flight of stairs.
- **long, deep, slow** breaths, the emphasis is on controlling your breathing. As the surges build in intensity you may find your rate of breathing increases, this is normal. As your muscles work harder your

body needs more oxygen to keep everything working effectively, but **retain control – finding a sense of rhythm in your breath will help you to maintain control**.

- Make a deep open-throat sound to help you focus as you exhale – e.g. ahh, ooo, hmm
- Try counting the number of breaths that you take during a surge to maintain your focus on your breathing (this is also a Zen meditation technique).
- repeat this type of breathing as many times as necessary for length of each surge – **never** hold your breath or over exert your breathing.
- focus your attention on your rising abdomen. Visualise the cervix drawing up and open.
- Think about how your breath is providing your body the oxygen it needs to work hard and also providing your baby with oxygen to keep him/her safe and calm – if you are not breathing, essentially, your baby will not be breathing either.
- your body is completely loose and limp, totally relaxed.
- Practice during Braxton Hicks surges, during leg cramps, when trying to ignore an itch or other annoying or uncomfortable sensation.

BIRTH BREATHING:

Used when **breathing your baby down** during the second stage (the 'pushing' stage).

- **Inhale**: take quick, deep breath in.
- **exhale**: breathe down to your baby (to the count of 10 if you like) strongly and slowly. Visualise the cervix opening up and the birth path ready, like the petals of a rose, folding outward as your baby moves down to the perineal opening. The breath can be released slowly from your mouth or nose, a long, slow, gentle stream of air

releasing the pressure from your head and body and maintaining the circulation of oxygen to your body and your baby.
- let the energy from your breath flow down through your body to your birth path.
- as you get closer to crowning you will feel the pressure and the sensation similar to when you need to move your bowels – this means that your baby is in the correct position for birth. Visualise your breathing sending love and energy down to your baby and to the places your body needs it- down and out. NB. the only time a panting breath is used is when the head is crowning, your midwife or doctor may instruct you to **pant** for the rest of that surge so the baby's head eases out gently.
- Practice this breathing each day when you use your bowels (great for relieving constipation!)

BASIC PHYSICAL RELAXATION TECHNIQUES

To practice relaxation on your own or *with your partner*, you need to be comfortable. Collect a bunch of pillows and show your partner where you like them. Do these exercises in various positions: standing and leaning against your partner, leaning over a fit-ball or the back of a chair, sitting down, lying on your side, and even on all-fours; this way you wont be limited to lying on your back to relax during labour.

Progressive Relaxation

This classic technique usually involves tensing and then relaxing each muscle group in your body. However, the technique shown here is a more passive method focusing on breathing and deep relaxation.

Keeping your breathing slow and rhythmic, focus on each part of your body in turn, allowing the muscles to relax fully and the tension to melt away. As you breathe in imagine breathing in relaxation and as you exhale, imagine all of the tension etc leaving your body.

Technique: Use the Relaxation tracks on your **CD** or ask your partner to work with you using the following script.

Preparation: This script is very helpful when you are first learning physical relaxation, it is a basic and easy to follow script that helps ease you gently into deep relaxation. You will be interested to find that with only a small amount of practice you will be able to go very quickly and easily into relaxation.

When you first start with this script try it a few times in the same week to get a good feel for it. After a couple of weeks or once you feel that you are able to go easily into deep physical relaxation move on to the next script.

Work: this script can be a useful reminder during labour of how easily and quickly you are able to drift down into relaxation, allowing all of the muscles in your body to release and relax, let all of your muscles be loose and limp.

Progressive Relaxation Script

Begin by asking your partner to sit or lie in a comfortable position with arms and legs un-crossed, offer them pillows or cushions for support. Remind your partner to think about their breathing and to use the relaxation breathing technique, breathing in to the count of 4 and out for 6 or 8 or simply taking a deep sigh.

Just allow your eyes to gently close. Don't force them shut. Just allow your eyelids to gently meet and feel how comfortable it is to just sit with your eyes gently closed. In a few moments you will be in one of the most relaxed states you have ever known. You'll continue to hear the sound of my voice and other sounds around you but none of these will interfere with your ability to go very deeply into relaxation. Place your awareness on your becoming increasingly relaxed.

Now place your awareness back to your eyes and feel all of the little muscles in and around your eyes relaxing, and as the muscles around your eyes relax, you become aware that your eyelids are closing even more thoroughly. And as your eyelids close more thoroughly all of the little worry lines around your eyes begin to fade and disappear. And now it seems that your eyelids are closing more tightly, so much so that it seems they are beginning to feel as though they were sealed shut. As though there was some kind of glue on the edges of your eyelids. Your eyes feel locked shut.

Feel how comfortable it is to sit with your eyes closed and with that wonderful feeling of relaxation beginning to drift through your body.

Allow the wave of relaxation to gently drift down and around your cheeks and into your jaw, around your mouth, and feel the relaxation cause your lower jaw to become heavy and drop.

Now the relaxation begins to drift through and around your neck and the top of your shoulders. You feel the muscles in your shoulders becoming loose and limp. So relaxed that your shoulders just want to sink into the frame of your body. Just relax and let go.

Now the relaxation drifts down and across your upper arms, your elbows, your lower arms and all the way down to your wrists. Your arms are relaxing and becoming limp. And now from your wrists all the way down to the tips of your fingers, your hands feel so very relaxed. Place all of your awareness on the growing relaxation in your hands and arms, fingers so relaxed that they begin to feel larger and numb. You might be finding that your hands are tingling with numbness. Or perhaps there is a strange kind of floating feeling, almost as if your hands were not there at all, not up, not down, just comfortable and total relaxation.

And now allow that same level of total relaxation to flow down through your body, every muscle, every nerve and every cell throughout your entire body, like a series of dominoes, gently tilted, drift d o w n, d o w n, d o w n, as you find yourself going deeper and deeper into relaxation.

Now let that wonderful wave of relaxation move down through your stomach and into your abdomen. As the relaxation flows into your abdomen, take a moment to focus your awareness and imagine our baby floating in pure relaxation, completely protected from stress and tension. Free from fear and aware only of how very much _____ (insert he/she/they as appropriate) are loved. I am going to be quiet for a moment now as you picture our baby, calm and comfortable.

(Pause for a few moments to allow your partner – and perhaps yourself – to picture your baby.)

And now allow the relaxation to flow into your pelvic area, releasing tension from your pelvic floor and letting the warm, soft flow of relaxation drift down into your legs. Feel your legs becoming loose and limp, totally relaxed and comfortable. Allow that pleasant feeling of relaxation to drift all the way down through your legs until your legs feel heavy, heavier and heavier, like logs of wood.

And now allow the relaxation to flow around your ankles and your feet and into the soles of your feet, right to the very tips of your toes. Feel the soft tingling of relaxation all through the soles of your feet. Totally relaxed and ready to allow your mind to go where it will. As you bring yourself deeper and deeper into this comfortable state of total relaxation.

(pause and allow your partner to enjoy this feeling)

Now as you sit totally relaxed, you are free to see yourself easily and comfortably birthing your baby. See how happy you are at the thought that your baby will soon be with you. Know how calm and comfortable you are in your birthing body, and how confident you are in your ability to bring your baby into this world. Your relaxation allows you to work with nature to birth your beautiful baby, safely and comfortably.

(pause and allow your partner to visualise this scene)

(you can skip the next section if your partner would like to remain in this calm and relaxed state and drift off to sleep or if you are using this script during labour)

In a moment, I will count you up from 1 to 5 and, as I do, you will feel the energy coming back into your body – mind alert and refreshed.....1.....2.....3.....coming up slowly.....4.....becoming aware of your surroundings, the sounds around you, the feeling of your clothes on your skin.....5.....mentally alert, physically energised and spiritually calm.

PRE-NATAL BONDING

Parents need to begin active parenting during pregnancy because, even at this very early stage, babies are developing more rapidly than previously thought possible. From the second month of pregnancy, research and observations reveal that your baby is cognitively active, with a rapidly developing sensory system, which permits highly tuned sensitivity and responsiveness. Long before the development of advanced brain structures, unborn babies are seen interacting with each other (in the case of twins) and learning from experience. They seem especially interested in the larger environment provided by mother and father, and react to individual voices, stories, music, and even simple interaction games with parents. Principally the parents determine the quality of the uterine environment so it is very important to think about the environment that your baby is living in during pregnancy.

This means that pregnancy is a time to think not only about your health and nutrition, about the foods and medications that you ingest, about quitting smoking and giving up alcohol – but you also need to think about the psychological environment your baby is developing in.

How much stress do you experience during your day? This is the same amount of stress your baby is experiencing. When you are stressed your body releases catecholamines (the same hormone released in fight or flight) this hormone flows through your body and across the placenta and through to your baby, creating the same physiological responses in your baby's little body as in your own – tense muscles, increased heartbeat and respiratory rate etc. What is this teaching your baby? Your baby is learning from any repeated stressor and developing an association between the sounds of stressful events and the unpleasant feelings of begin stressed – your baby will be born with this knowledge, that this event, person or other stimuli is a source of stress.

Happily, the reverse is also true – any event, person or other stimuli that brings about feelings of love, calmness or relaxation for you will be providing these feelings for your baby, again through hormonal communication. Spending quality time with your partner during pregnancy is thus essential to the development of pre-natal love between father and baby. Each time baby hears Dad's voice at the same time as receiving the endorphins released by Mum's body the association between Dad and feeling good will be strengthened and reinforced- your baby will be born loving their Daddy. You can use this same understanding for developing a pre-natal relationship between your baby and any significant other – an older child or grandparent for example.

In a famous experiment by Anthony DeCasper and colleagues at the University of North Carolina, Greensboro, mothers read the Dr. Seuss story, The Cat In the Hat, at regular intervals before birth. At birth, babies were exposed to recordings, which they could select by sucking on a non-nutritive nipple. After a few trials, babies cleverly sucked at whatever speed was necessary to obtain their mother's voice reading "The Cat in the Hat. Similarly, in utero, musical passages repeated regularly--such as theme music for the soap opera Neighbours or the bassoon passage from Peter and the Wolf--are identified and preferred immediately after birth. In a recent experiment, French mothers repeated a children's rhyme each day from week 33 to week 37 of gestation. At the end of this time (still inside the womb) the babies showed memory and learning for this particular rhyme as opposed to similar rhymes they had not heard. (Chamberlain, 2002).

As early as 450 BC the Chinese were aware of the need for special childbearing treatment. They believed that the health, dietary, emotional, and environmental stimuli (including music) that a pregnant mother was exposed to had an effect on the growing fetus

Your Baby's First Lessons

The ancient Chinese had an art they called Taikyo. Mothers practiced Taikyo by talking to, massaging and singing to their unborn children. They believed that Taikyo would make their children smarter and provide them with an intellectual and emotional head start. As with so many things, we now know that this ancient practice worked. Parents of all cultures have talked, sung, and played music to their unborn children for centuries. For most, this has been little more than a way to bond with their child before they are born. Modern science is now discovering that unborn children benefit from this stimulation in ways never imagined.

During the last trimester of pregnancy, as well as early childhood, children lose a significant number of brain cells. These cells atrophy or "die" much like a muscle if it is not used. If we can stimulate or "turn-on" these important cells, a child's brain is strengthened for life. Throughout life, this early advantage means that the enriched child will be better able to absorb and appreciate far more of their environment than a child who did not receive this advantage. This first "prenatal classroom" now becomes more important than any other classroom. Your baby's world inside the womb prepares her for life outside by providing a wide range of experiences that are crucial to her cognitive and sensory development. During the last trimester, she's eavesdropping on your conversations, discerning the differences between male and female voices, and monitoring your moods. In fact, during the final months, most of your baby's movements-as well as increases in her heart rate- are in response to specific noises, touches, changes in light, and other sensations.

Techniques: The techniques for prenatal bonding really are as boundless as your imagination, some common techniques used include:

- **Reading a story** (preferably the same story) to your baby every night, Mum and Dad can take it in turns or this might be Dad's special story that will bring calm and comfort to your child after birth.
- **Make up a special poem or little song** to say or sing to your baby everyday, you might like to write it down so you can give it to your child when they are older.
- **Play the kick-poke game** – every time you baby starting moving around say "kick baby kick" and gently press into the place where your baby has just kicked. By repeating this every time your baby kicks, within a few days, or sooner, your baby will have developed an association between kicking and hearing your voice and will begin to kick just to hear back from you!

Follow the light – find a torch that is strong enough to shine through the palm of your hand and place it onto your belly near where you think your baby's head is positioned. Slowly move the torch around and wait to see if your baby responds by kicking into the light and following it around.

Any stimuli that you find calming and relaxing will have the same effect on your baby and repeated exposure will strengthen their association. Find something that will be helpful to you as a parent, a song or story for example, that is easy to repeat and sign or read to your baby, even when you are feeling tired or sleep deprived. Despite claims on internet e-commerce sites and in other places, there is no hard science in choosing a song that is right for you and your baby – we use *Twinkle, Twinkle Little Star* – I know it well and can sing it in my sleep – over and over and over if necessary – it works wonders!

Preparation: This is probably very obvious, but just in case...choose your bonding activity and repeat as often as possible during pregnancy – especially from 28 weeks onwards, when your baby's hearing is fully developed. By repeating your bonding activity every day your baby will develop a strong association between the stimuli that you are using and feeling calm, loved and relaxed, you will be developing an invaluable parenting tool, you will be teaching your baby that the world is a nice place to live and creating a strong foundation for one of the most important relationships in your life.

Work: Expose your baby to your chosen bonding activity as soon as practical after birth. You might like to sing your special song to your baby during the first breast feed or even during second stage of labour as your baby is actually birthing. You will be welcoming your child into an already familiar and comforting environment.

An important message of the research findings is that memory and learning seem to be an integral part of life, including the first nine months in utero. Life in the uterus is extremely active and interactive, just like any other classroom.

This script is primarily for use as a pregnancy relaxation – words from the script can be used as prompts during labour.

Loving Welcome Relaxation Script

Begin with progressive or rapid relaxation or other well practiced 'lead in' then add the following script in once deep relaxation has been achieved.

And now that you have reached this very relaxed state you feel almost as though you are leaving your body behind…floating away on a gentle wave of relaxation

And as you rest in this totally relaxed, deeply comfortable state, you are free, free of all fear and tension, free to see yourself easily and comfortably birth your baby. And as you breathe fully and deeply, feel your breath going down to your baby, helping your baby in the journey it has to make.

Feel the confidence and assurance, feel the calmness and the peace, most of all, feel the love with which you are going to welcome your baby into this world.

And as you see your baby surrounded by your love, protected by your relaxation, in your mind's eye, see yourself talking to your baby, welcoming your baby, guiding your baby in the journey that you are going to make together, your body, your baby, at one with nature.

Drifting calmly and peacefully through your journey on a wave of relaxation. Soon your baby will be with you, what a wonderful and joyous occasion. Focus on welcoming your baby, calmly, confidently and comfortably. Bring your awareness to how you are already creating a loving, welcoming environment for your baby.

[To finish, count up from 1 to 5 slowly or for sleep or during labour leave your partner in this deeply relaxed state .]

IMAGERY AND VISUALISATION

Visualisation can be used during pregnancy and birthing to help with relaxation, to focus and redirect attention and to aid the body in the natural processes of birthing.

During visualisation you take thoughts and experiences and translate them into mental images that can help you reach your birthing goals. The idea of using pictures in your mind to manage your physical reality may sound abstract, but think about how imagining fresh baked cookies or some other yummy food can make you hungry.

During **pregnancy** many women visualise <u>a safe place</u> from their memory or imagination that gives them a sense of well-being. This might be your favourite place in nature, your favourite holiday destination, at home; any of these may be real or imagined (*The Gentle Surge Relaxation on the CD is great for this*). It is very important to also take time to visualise <u>your baby</u> during pregnancy. Initiate relaxation using the Progressive or Rapid Relaxation technique and take yourself deep within, to the place when your baby is growing, in mind and body. Imagine sending all of your love and energy down through your body to your baby. Imagine your baby floating comfortably in the soft mist of your relaxation, protected from any stress or tension from the outside world. If you are familiar with the charkas you may like to imagine a soft mist of each of the colours of the <u>rainbow</u>. Allow them to permeate your body in harmony with your charkas (or use *the Rainbow Charka Script* following).

During **birthing**, visualizing images of the cervix <u>opening</u> or other opening images (like flowers blossoming or ripples in a pond) may be effective to help labour progress (rose buds and the lotus seem to be the two most favored flowers for this visualisation). A great 'place to be' during birthing is in your '<u>control room</u>' the place deep within your mind where the sub-conscious controls all of the processes and systems of your body. Here, you can turn off sensations, focus on other feelings or change your experience depending on the 'settings' that you choose on your control panel (*practice with the Connecting Mind & Body track on your CD*).

You might like to try the <u>Grounded Tree</u> visualisation during the more intense part of the first stage of birthing; imagine your feet grounded in the earth as if they were tree roots deeply implanted, strong and unmoving. Imagine your spine strong and sturdy like a tree trunk, holding you steady, unwavering in your love for your baby and your trust in your body. Imagine your arms and legs like the branches, swaying gently in the breeze, hands and feet as loose and limp as the soft leaves. Imagine that your mind is the clear blue sky surrounding the tree, a gentle breeze blowing through to clear your thoughts as they come and go. And your partner is the sun, providing nurturing, supporting warmth, feel the love radiating from this special person.

Another useful visualisation during surges is to imagine yourself <u>on a beach</u> using the mental image of the rolling waves to carry you through each surge. You might imagine diving under the waves or standing in the shallow water and jumping the small waves as they roll into shore (especially effective for experienced Mums who have actually done this with older children). Experience the waves as the energy of the water, the rising and falling movement or as a refreshing relief from the heat of the sun.

Any image or mental picture that contributes to your overall sense of wellbeing is going to be useful as a visualisation during pregnancy and birthing. The goal is to focus your mind and your awareness on the calming and strengthening aspects of the image and use the feelings generated to relax your mind and trust that your body knows how to birth your baby.

The idea of using pictures in your mind to manage your physical reality may sound abstract, but think about how imagining fresh baked cookies or some other yummy food can make you hungry or salivate. The strong connection between mind and body makes visualisation a powerful birthing tool for ensuring the body is receiving messages from a calm and relaxed mind.

Sports psychologists use mental imagery or visualisation to help athletes perform.

Technique: Determine the thoughts and scenes you find most relaxing and practice meditating on them frequently throughout your pregnancy, especially in the final few weeks. You may find one the following scenes helpful: rolling waves, waterfalls, meandering streams, walking along the beach with your partner. Think of your favourite place in nature – this will probably be a source of good feelings for you and you will therefore find it quite easy to 'go there' in your imagination.

Think about images for use during surges. When a surge begins, you might find it helpful to picture your uterus actually working, drawing the cervix open and up during first stage. Alternatively it might work better for you to connect the imagery with your breath and imagine blowing away a boat on a lake as you breathe through each surge.

Close your eyes and focus on the positive, effective part of each surge. Each surge bringing you closer to holding your baby, each one only a few breaths long, working to bring your baby gently into the world.

Preparation: Practice your visualisations and breathing techniques together during pregnancy to develop a strong association for deep relaxation during labour.

Use the *Gentle Surge* and other relaxation tracks on your **CD**, one at a time is enough. Try to listen to one every day from 34 weeks onwards or ask your partner to help you with the scripts in this book.

Work: Use your chosen and practiced visualisation to help you into deep relaxation.

During surges, especially the more intense ones, focus on your visualisation and allow it to fill your mind so that nothing else is able to take over your thoughts. Remember that good visualisation is not just about closing your eyes but also imagining that you can feel, smell, touch and hear the things that you are imagining – make them real. A well chosen and practiced visualisation will enable you to either transcend beyond your surges or to work even more effectively and efficiently with them – your choice.

Triumph Meditation – For Fear Release

Spend some time imagining that you have already had the wonderful birth that you are preparing for. If you want to be free of any fear or anxiety about giving birth, imagine that you are already completely at ease with the process:

- Use a physical relaxation technique to go deeply into relaxation. Allow yourself to become quiet and still. Just before sleep or first thing in the morning are excellent times.
- Create every detail you can in this future moment when you are totally at ease and experiencing a wonderful birth. The colours, the emotion, the smells, the physical sensations. Make it real! Your subconscious does NOT know the difference between a real and an imagined event.
- Put yourself into this future moment and feel it as a NOW moment. Use any insight from this experience to prepare you for the next one, the one where you will actually get to hold your new baby. Do this by collecting information about yourself, your reactions, emotions and behaviours in this future moment and using them to guide you through the next.
- Look back at the past from this future moment. Notice what it feels like to know that the old or unwanted experience is in the past. Allow yourself to feel as if that experience happened long ago and focus on how good you feel about this new experience.

- Do it again. Spend just five minutes once or twice a day in this state with this new belief and it will begin to plant the seeds necessary to create change. It will help to quiet the self-defeating inner voice that used to try to tell you that you couldn't do it, and you will notice changes in your physical body that will support the mental change.

Rainbow Chakra Script

Initiate relaxation with the Progressive Relaxation script or by using the Rapid Relaxation Technique (5,4,3,2,1)

Now in this beautifully relaxed state, your mind is free to imagine a magnificent rainbow with each of the colours shimmering in harmony with the energy of life. Your body is filled with life, the energy of your body and your baby connecting in this miracle.

Allow your body now to absorb the energy of the rainbow. Let the soft mist of each of the colours permeate your entire body bringing you confidence and assurance. Allow the mist to drift around you and as you breathe it in, imagine the strength and vitality it provides your baby.

The mist of the rainbow draws away all tension leaving you calm and at peace. And you are able go deeper and deeper into relaxation.

Picture yourself now surrounded by a soft red mist, a mist that gently swirls around your feet and legs. Taking away all tension, all fear.

Bathing you in soft, gentle relaxation. Allow the red mist of perfect relaxation drift throughout all of your body.

As you relax within this mist your trust in your strength and your body's ability to birth your baby grows. You draw this strength from the earth, totally stable and secure. Guided in this journey, so natural, so perfectly natural.

You have all the energy you need to birth your baby just as nature intended. Relax totally in the knowledge that you feel strong and confident and sure that your body can birth your baby easily.

Now, in your mind's eye, see yourself on a mist of soft, orange. Your body feels relaxed as the orange mist surrounds you, and your pelvis softens as the orange mist drifts around you.

The orange mist is like a sponge, absorbing all tension, soaking it up and away from you, bathing you in the soft mist of peace, relaxation and comfort.

This orange mist reminds you of the knowledge your body carries, the wisdom it needs to do its job effortlessly and allow your baby to be born. You are able to give birth easily and safely and you deserve to do so. Relax totally in the knowledge that your body knows how to birth your baby.

Now see yourself in your mind's eye the yellow mist of natural relaxation. Your abdomen becomes calm and peaceful as the yellow mist drifts around you.

With each breath that you take breathe in this soft yellow mist of calmness you go even deeper into relaxation. This gentle yellow mist has the ability to draw away all of your fears and anxieties. In this mist of soft yellow, you are able to release and let go, fully and completely.

Your mind is calm and fearless, completely trusting. You joyfully await your baby's birth, and with each breath, each surge, you move closer and closer to meeting your baby.

Now as you breathe gently, a soft green mist envelops you. You breathe in this soft green mist, and the entire area of your chest and particularly your heart relax more deeply than ever relaxed before. Within this green mist you open your heart and your life to even greater love. Your heart beats in harmony to the colour green, you feel completely filled with peace and love.

All the love for your baby comes to you in this place, you wrap your arms around your baby, thanking them for helping you open to such pure love. Within this love you find a gift, a gift of trust, that you are not alone on this journey of your baby's birth. Your baby is there every step of the way awaiting your loving welcome.

Now picture yourself in a beautiful blue mist and feel your throat and neck open and relax. The throat and neck soften within the blue mist, so breathe in the blue mist and feel all tension melting away.

And in this wonderful state of relaxation your find a way to express all your needs. Letting go of expectations and opening your mind to this wonderful journey. Your decisions regarding your birth are easily made and those around you support you in your choices. You are loved and nurtured, just as your baby is loved and nurtured

And now see a beautiful mist of soft violet swirling in around you. A soft, sweet colour that puts your mind at ease, because the mind is relaxed and open within the colour of violet.

Sense the gentle confident thoughts that begin to fill your mind as the mist of violet helps you to let go.

Your wisdom flows freely within the violet mist, you intuitively know what is right for you and your baby. Your natural birthing instinct is within you and you know that it is right to hand your birthing over to your body and your baby.

And now, perfectly relaxed, see yourself on a mist of pure white. All of the colours of the rainbow surrounding you with peace and tranquility. Sense the feelings of confidence that are developing day by day as you embrace the knowledge that birthing is a natural process of mind and body working together with your spirit. Imagine the white mist filling you as you breathe deeply and fully. And as you breathe out, release and let go.

Your mind, your body and your baby will work in harmony just as they are designed to do, so natural, nothing to remember. Let the white mist permeate every part of you while you continue to grow in confidence that this will indeed be a calm, gentle and welcoming birth.

In a moment, I will very slowly count you up from 1 to 5 and, as I do, you will feel the energy gradually coming back into your body, refreshed and confident.

Be aware of your breathing and the wonderfully relaxed state your body is in…

Coming up slowly

Fingers and toes beginning to move as the energy returns to your body.

Coming up slowly

Aware of the sounds around you, aware of the feeling of your clothes on your skin

In your own time

Remembering the room that you are in and the time of day. Bringing with you the calmness and confidence of your inner mind.

In your own time, and when you are ready, totally trusting in your ability to birth your baby, you can open your eyes. Awake and refreshed.

Partners:

If your partner has chosen a visualisation that you are familiar with, e.g. your favourite holiday together or a favourite place in nature that you have also been to, you can help your partner by offering suggestions of the things that you can see, hear, smell, feel or even taste – this can be especially helpful if she is having trouble focusing despite being physically relaxed. Try something that's really specific and vivid for you both….

Example - my husband's and my favourite meal from our favourite holiday in this wonderful little restaurant on a tiny little man-made lake near the beach…mmmmmm….

Go on to provide as much detail about taste, colour and smell as possible….mmmmmm.

MASSAGE

Just like visualisation, massage can work to occupy your conscious mind with a pleasant stimulus and block the sensory gate in the brain stem. It also encourages the release of endorphins and creates closeness between you and your partner during labour and birthing.

Massage can be any form of pleasant touch that you like. Here are some suggestions for what might be helpful during labour and birthing.

Partners:

Warning!!!

The woman you know now, who looooooves massage and takes whatever she can get…might not be the same woman you are with in labour. In labour this woman might not want anyone touching her and could be very forthright in telling you so – take a few of those relaxation type breaths and a few steps back…

Touch Relaxation

Technique - This technique involves working with a partner to identify tense areas of the body. Most people have a certain area where they tend to store tension. Learn what it is. You may clench your jaw, or rub your temples or make fists. Study your partner for these areas and by firmly touching or stroking that area, encourage relaxation there.

Find a cue (touch, verbal or something else) that you can agree to use. The least relaxing thing in the world is when someone commands you to "RELAX!" With a soothing voice use words that describe a relaxed state like soft, melt, flow, warm, loose, limp, release, smooth, let go and anything else you can think of.

If you are using touch as your cue, imagine your muscles melting into your partner's touch or that your partner's hand is able to draw out any tension leaving you totally relaxed. Use your breath to help with this.

Preparation – Practice will ensure that the cue you and your partner have chosen will be effective during labour. Remember – more practice leads to a stronger association, a stronger association leads to a more effective technique. You can also incorporate the relaxation breathing into this technique to help develop the association between the deep sigh-type breath and physical relaxation.

> **Partners:**
>
> This technique is especially good for helping partners to develop sensitivity to tension in the pregnant mum's body. This heightened awareness of the level of relaxation in the woman's body will help you to know when she needs your help during labour.

Work - During labour, especially just after a surge has released, ask your partner to use the cue that you have established to help you identify and release any tension that may have built up during the surge.

Light Touch Massage

The light touch massage is based on the same principle as a TENS machine. The goal is to overwhelm the central nervous system, running up and down the spine, with a very pleasant and tingly sensation. This technique is also designed to stimulate the release of endorphins and minimise any discomfort. So not only are any pain messages blocked out of the brain stem by the numerous messages about the sensation of the massage, but you will also have the benefits of endorphins blocking the pain receptors in the brain – a double whammy!

Technique: Requires a partner – who will use a very light touch over the back, neck, breasts and upper arms. The feather-light touch produces an overwhelming sensation, stimulating the nerves in the back and neck. Your partner is aiming to produce that tingly kind of feeling – shivers up your spine.

Use a repetitive feather light stroke, applied simultaneously to both sides of the spine/back, over the entire area of the back and neck using either or both or the following techniques (or your own version):

Using a very light stroke in an upward 'V' motion, beginning at the very base of the spine, the sacrum and very gradually moving up the spine and out to the sides (and around to the nipple area if privacy permits) until the stroke goes all the way from the base of the spine, up the spine and around behind the ears and all the way back down. Therefore, the first of your strokes will be quite a flat 'V' shape, the strokes will gradually become bigger with each new movement until your last stroke is a very long tall 'V'. Use the backs of your fingers, your fingernails, for the up & outwards motion and your fingertips for the down & back motion.

Using a very light stroke in a sideways '8' (infinity symbol) or cross-over motion, begin the sequence at the hips, bring the fingers (using the back of the fingers, the fingernails) in towards the spine, past each other and extend the cross-over motion through so that your arms are crossed-over and each hand is at the opposite hip from which it started. Now reverse the motion so that the hands cross back to their original position. Continue this motion all the way up the back to the base of the skull, remembering to include the upper arms and breasts/nipples (if possible and desired) in your massage.

Preparation: ...partners need LOTS and LOTS of practice to do this one well... Seriously though, any relaxation and associated release of endorphins during pregnancy is going to benefit your baby.

Work:
- To manage discomfort – use during a surge.
- To help deepen relaxation – use between surges in conjunction with physical relaxation (e.g. the progressive or rapid relaxation techniques)

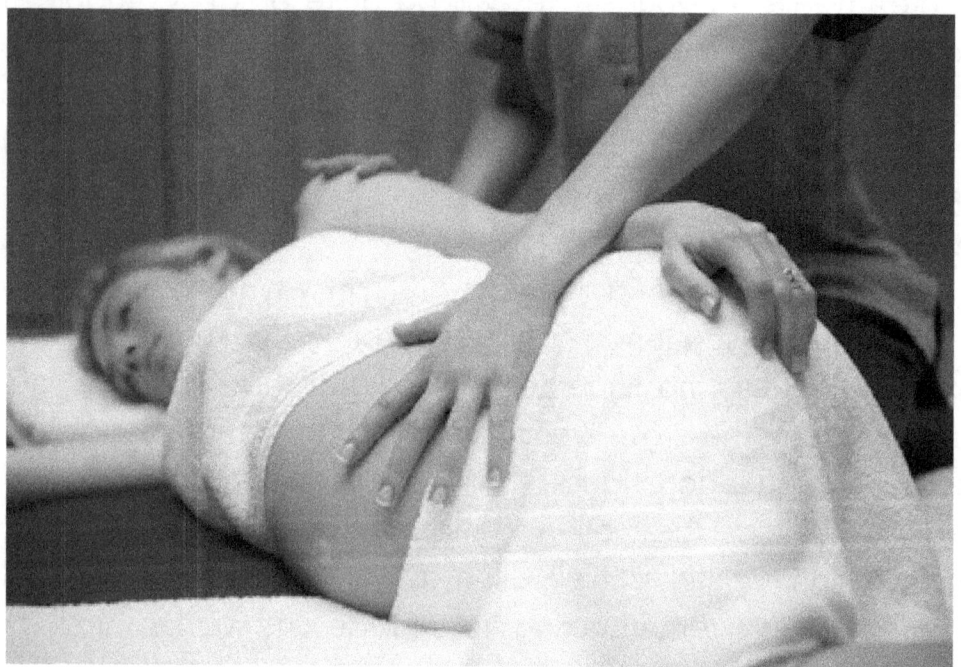

How does massage help relieve pain?

Massage stimulates the body to release endorphins which are natural pain-killing and mood-lifting substances. Endorphins are responsible for the 'feel-good' factor — the 'high' you feel after vigorous exercise, or a good laugh with your friends. In labour, massage is important because it brings you close to the person who is caring for you, be this your midwife or your birth companion. The touch of someone who loves you and wants to help you is very empowering when your surges are at their strongest and you are perhaps tired and finding it hard to relax.

Are massage oils a good idea?

Using oil makes massage easier to carry out and more pleasant to receive. However, you have to be careful which oil you choose for labour. Don't buy an essential oil without consulting an aromatherapist or naturopath. Essential oils can be very powerful substances and can interfere with surges if used wrongly. Some aromatherapists prefer just to use a base oil for labour. Base oils include sweet almond and grapeseed. Don't use sweet almond if you have a nut allergy or are worried about nut allergies. Just as good is grapeseed and even a light olive oil which is particularly well absorbed by the skin.
See the natural therapies section in the appendix for some suggestions about essential oils.

Labour Massage

In addition to the 'Touch Relaxation' and 'Light Touch' massage, the following massage techniques can be used during the birthing process. Whichever technique you choose, remember to communicate with your partner to ensure the massage is pleasant and beneficial.

Shoulder massage

It's important for you to keep you shoulders relaxed during labour. Relaxed shoulders assist rhythmic breathing and rhythmic breathing maximises the oxygen available to both you and your baby. Ask your partner to massage your shoulders to help your shoulders stay relaxed and keep your breathing at just the right rate.

Technique - place your hands on the mum's shoulders and lean lightly on them. This will help her drop her shoulders if they are 'hunched' with tension. Next, stroke down from the shoulders to her elbows, maintaining a rhythmical action and applying firm pressure. Use your hands in a way that is telling her to *release* and *let go*, in a fairly directive manner. Ask her whether the massage is helping and if there is a way you could make it better.

You could also try resting your fingers on top of her shoulders and using your thumbs to massage in small firm circles behind the shoulder blades. Ask if you are pressing too hard or not hard enough, and make sure you are massaging with slow rhythmical stroke. It's important to avoid frantic massage as this serves only to speed up her breathing when the aim is to slow it down!

Back massage

Many women feel surges strongly in their lower back, so back massage is very useful.

Technique - In the early part of the first stage of labour, you can use a flat hand to stroke down the side of her spine, from shoulder to bottom. Then use the other hand to stroke down the other side of her spine, maintaining a rhythmical movement, with one hand constantly in contact with your partner's back. These long, slow strokes are very soothing. Make sure that you use the whole of your hand and not just the heel of your palm. Your fingers need to be in contact with her body so that you may respond to any tension you find. If you are also using the Touch Relaxation technique you might like to use the two techniques in conjunction, pausing at the end or beginning of each stroke.

In the latter part of the first stage of labour, you can use the heel of your palm to massage firmly over the base of her spine (right down low, just on or above the separation of the buttocks), use both hands, one over or on top of the other so that you have the strength of both arms focused on the one spot. Apply quite a lot of pressure to counteract the strong surges. Imagine you have a tennis ball in the palm of your hand, apply the pressure you would need to hold it against your partner's back and roll the imaginary ball around the base of her spine.

Or use your thumbs to make deep circles over the dimples in her back, just over the hips at the top, outer part of the buttocks. Or simply find the bumpy part of the hips bones on her lower back and press in here. Ask her what she is finding most helpful and adjust your movements accordingly. This is a technique that should be trialed a few times during the last few weeks of pregnancy to see which spots feel best or offer the most relief and benefit. As always, communication is the key to effective massage.

Foot massage

Many people who say that they can't tolerate having their feet touched nonetheless enjoy firm, rhythmical foot massage. The massage does need to be firm, however, or it will be unbearably ticklish. If you find yourself sitting down or in bed for long periods of your labour, foot massage is ideal. Your partner can simply stroke your feet firmly from ankle to toes, or make firm circles with his thumbs all over the soles of your feet. You may find that your feet become very cold in labour, and a foot massage will help to warm them up. Use a moisturiser cream rather than oil to make the massage easier, most people find that cream has a much better consistency for foot massage and also doesn't make the bottom of the feet slippery when rubbed in completely.

> **Partners** – if you are giving a foot massage during labour (or pregnancy!) please make sure any cream used is fully rubbed in to avoid the woman slipping when she stands up. It might even be best to get a warm face cloth and gently wipe the bottom of her feet when you have finished the massage.

Hand and Arm massage

If you have had an epidural and are lying in bed, shoulder or back massage might be almost impossible. And if you can't feel your feet, there's no point in your partner offering you a foot massage. In these circumstances, hand and arm massage is very soothing. Your partner can simply stroke each hand in turn, first on the back, then on the palm, sweeping firmly down from your wrist to your fingertips. He can make small circles all over your palm, and gently pull each finger in turn to release the tension. Then take the light touch massage up and down the arm – all the way to the base of the skull. This is a lovely way of being close to each other and making your labour special.

Not all women like massage...

If your birth companion is keen to massage you in labour, he may be very disappointed if you don't like it. However, some women simply cannot bear to be touched when they are focused on the birthing process. Other women find massage so helpful that they want their partners to keep rubbing their backs for hours on end! Partners need to be aware of these different reactions and respond accordingly.

AFFIRMATIONS

Using affirmations is a very simple and effective way of ensuring your mind-body connection is working to your advantage. Place a copy of the affirmations somewhere where you will see it regularly. It can be very powerful to write out your own, using your own words and desired phrases. Just remember to word the affirmations in the present and make them positive (i.e. avoid using *not* or *don't* type phrases).

Technique - two suggestions:

1. Listen to the *Birthing* Affirmations track on your CD. Choose a time when you are also occupied with something else, something relatively repetitive or mundane – ironing or doing the dishes for example (or something a little less domesticated – doing a puzzle maybe...?).

2. Choose 1 one of the statements to carry around in your mind. Think about the affirmation for as long as it takes for it to feel as if it 'belongs' in your mind and your system of beliefs. Some of the affirmations may instantly feel right and fit with the rest of your thinking, other may take a day or more to feel really comfortable and for you to truly *know* what it means (some might feel silly and wont work for you at all).

Preparation - Again, this really is just a matter of repetition and practice. Talk to your partner about the affirmations and what they mean to you and when you think about your birthing or talk to others about it, see if you can incorporate some aspects of the affirmations in the way you describe how your birthing is going to be and the good choices you and your partner have already made.

Work - Research has shown that most women who use birthing affirmations have found them particularly useful during the more intense part of the first stage of labour (Read, 2004). If you feel that your resolve and determination need strengthening at any time put on the affirmations track from the CD or ask your partner to remind you of your favourite affirmations and you will find yourself remembering just why you are doing all of this great work.

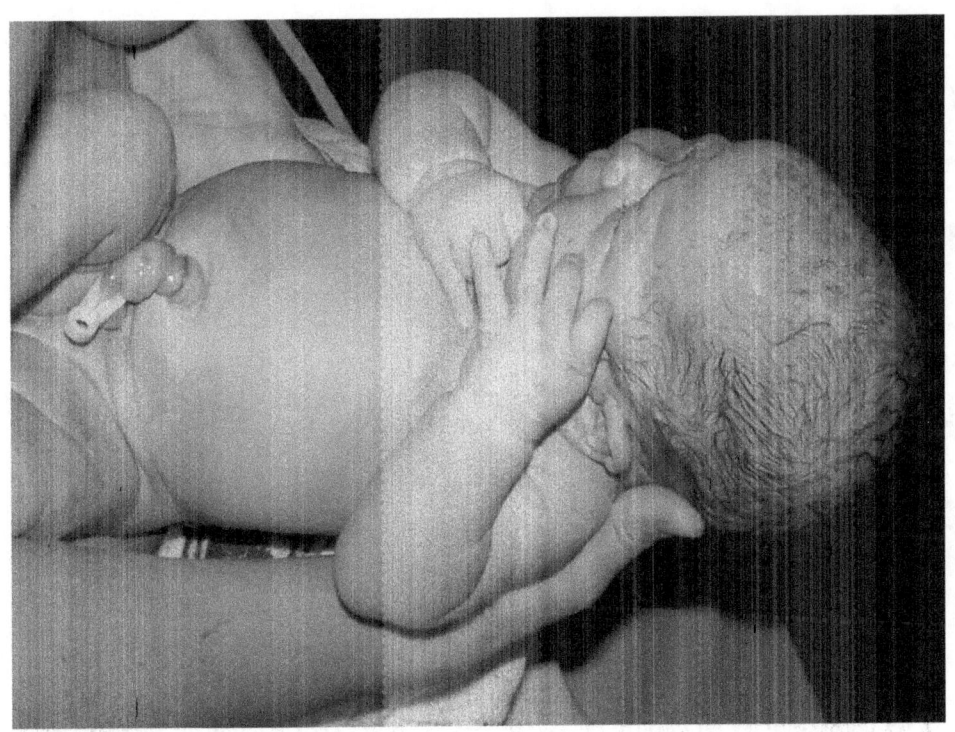

Affirmations

I am strong, I am confident, I am focused.

I release all fear as I prepare my mind and my body for the birth of my baby.

I am aware of my baby, and my baby's love for me.

My baby is surrounded by pure relaxation.

I am focused on a calm, welcoming birth.

I trust my body to know what it needs to do.

My mind is relaxed; my body is relaxed.

My muscles work in harmony to make birthing calm and comfortable.

I feel the endorphins flowing through my body, bringing me comfort.

I release and let go as my baby moves down.

My body opens comfortably and easily.

I allow my body to birth my baby.

I am empowered and know what is best for my baby.

My baby's birth will be welcoming because I am so calm and prepared.

I breathe deeply and fully, and release all tension.

My mind and body work as one.

I see my breath filling me with energising oxygen.

I feel and calm and confident, whatever turn my birthing takes.

I open my heart and my mind as I welcome my baby.

Each surge of my body brings my baby closer to me.

I deepen my relaxation as I move further into labour.

I trust my body.

My body remains loose and limp.

I meet each surge only with my breath; my body is at ease.

I see my healthy baby, safe in my arms.

I breathe slowly and fully through each wave.

I breathe loving energy, down to my baby.

My breath guides me through this journey.

I am connected to my baby, through love and trust.

With each breath I release and let go.

I am supported and nurtured as I birth my baby.

I feel my birthing energy fill my body as I birth my baby.

I am prepared and welcome my baby with calmness and with love.

I put all fear aside and welcome my baby with love and happiness.

Affirmations for an Awaiting Father

I have a very important role to play in the birth of my baby.

I feel so proud of what I am achieving.

I feel enormous love and warmth for my baby.

We are happy calm and peaceful.

I feel totally confident in my skills and instinct as a Dad.

I feel at ease with the needs of my baby.

I am feeling relaxed, content and at peace with the world.

My mind is still with calmness and love.

I act and speak in a manner that eases my partner into relaxation.

I meet each moment with confidence and calmness.

I want nothing more than health and happiness, for myself, and for my family.

I am present in every moment.

I am focused on a calm, comfortable birth for my baby and my partner.

I trust nature and my partner's body that knows what it needs to do.

I feel and calm and confident, whatever turn our birthing takes.

I put all fear aside and welcome my baby with love and happiness.

I have all the time I need to make the best decisions for my partner and my baby.

I am present in every moment.

RELAXATION DEEPENING TECHNIQUES

Rapid Relaxation Technique (5,4,3,2,1)

The *Rapid Relaxation Technique* is designed for use once you are feeling comfortable with the full body *Progressive Relaxation*. Once you are achieving a deep state of relaxation with the progressive script, move on to this faster, do-anywhere technique for achieving deep relaxation fast.

Practice at work, as a passenger in the car, during TV commercial breaks – anytime you would like to feel the benefits of being fully relaxed, quickly.

Technique - Imagine your body sectioned into 5 zones as outlined in the following picture.

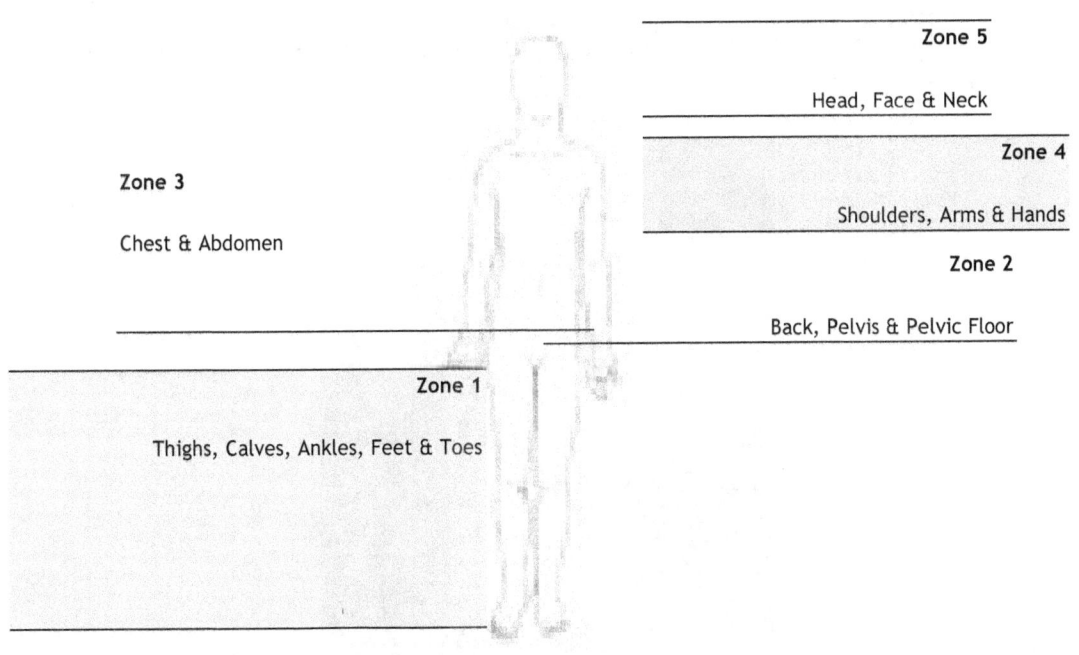

Take 2 or 3 deep sleep-sigh breaths. Count backwards to yourself from 5 down to 1, as you do, allow the muscles in each zone to relax respectively. Feel the tension slip away as the relaxation melts down through your body. Each number taking you deeper.

To enhance the experience, try counting each number as you exhale, still using the sleep-sigh breaths if you like.

Preparation - Practice as often as you like, the more you practice the easier and faster this technique will become, the deeper you will go. You might even find that you begin to forget to count.

Work - The technique will be especially useful:
- when your labour first begins as a quick reminder of your ability to relax deeply,
- in the car if you are travelling to the hospital,
- when you first arrive in your birthing suite and need to re-establish your relaxation, and
- after any distraction (e.g. Blood pressure being taken, monitoring baby's heart beat).

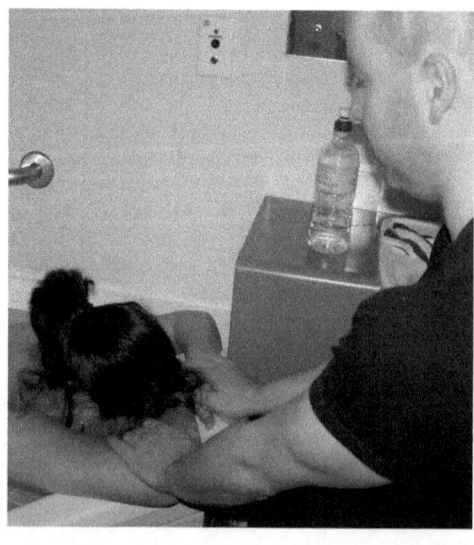

Birth Companion's Deepening Script

Partners - This script requires practice – mostly to get past the uncontrollable laughter set off by hearing your partner's hypnosis voice for the first few times….let the endorphins flow and stick with it. Use this script to deepen the level of relaxation during the later part of first stage. Don't worry if you are reading this script word for word the first few times or if it feels stiff and forced it will still have an effect on your partner. After a few practice runs the script will become familiar to you and you will be able to do it in your own words without reading this script and your movements will be more natural and flowing.

Ask your partner to find a comfortable position to sit or lie in. Sitting or standing to the side of your partner, holding hand open with palm facing your partner's abdomen, hand no more than a ruler's length away from their body, slowly raise your hand upward and say:

I'm going to pass my hand slowly upward in front of you, all the way to your head. When I reach your face, I want you to follow my hand only with your eyes…do not move your head. Very good. Now I want you to stare at my hand in a very dreamy kind of way, as though you can see right through it. As you do, your eyes begin to feel dry. You feel as though you want to blink. Your eyes are feeling quite tired now, as though they want to close. Please resist the temptation to close your eyes.

And now I'm going to slowly pass my hand down in front of your face; when I reach your eyes, just allow your eyelids to gently close and bring yourself into a deep, deep state of relaxation. **(pause)** deeply relaxed.

Now placing your awareness on your eyelids, it seems that your eyelids are closing more thoroughly. The muscles in and around your eyes are relaxing. Forehead smoothing out, and all of the little worry lines beginning to fade and disappear. Now it seems that your eyelids are sealed, and the same quality of total relaxation begins to drift down over your upper cheeks, your lower cheeks, your mouth, your upper and lower jaw. Your place your tongue behind your upper teeth, and your lower jaw recedes, as you go deeper, and still deeper. Releasing all of tension from your body. **(pause)**

Now I'm going to lift your arm at the wrist. Don't help me; let me do all the work; let your arm go limp; (lift arm about 30cm above the lap). Let me hold the weight of your arm **(pause)**. Now I'm going to drop your arm down onto your lap; when your arm drops down onto your leg, you'll bring yourself twice as deep as you are now. (release arm and let it drop) I'm going to lift your arm again and let it drop. As it drops onto your leg, you will double your relaxation again, and go deeper (repeat the lifting and dropping sequence). And once more, I'm going to lift your arm and drop it, and you'll go into an ultimate depth of relaxation – deeper than you've ever been (repeat the lifting and dropping sequence- If your partner doesn't like the lifting and dropping try applying pressure to her shoulder using the palm of your hand).

Now, as you rest, you are teaching your body how to thoroughly relax and go within, just as you'll do when you are bringing our baby into the world, turning your birthing over to your body, and letting go.

(Leave this next bit out if you are using this script during labour or if your partner would like to drift of to sleep.)

And now I'm going to count from one up to five. You'll begin to be aware of your surroundings, feeling mentally alert, physically energised and spiritually calm and confident. (Slowly) 1…..2…..hands beginning to move…..3…..4…..feet beginning to move…..5….. Awake and feeling good.

PREPARING YOUR BODY FOR BIRTHING

A stretching routine is very good for toning the perineal area, stretching ligaments, strengthening the inner thigh and abdominal muscles and promoting proper body alignment. A stretching routine could include the following stretches or something similar:

Toning, stretching and strengthening the back and abdominal muscles through yoga or other stretching routine and a moderate exercise program of walking or swimming will help your body prepare for the work and stretching that it will do during labour. It can also help to alleviate some of the discomforts of later pregnancy. In addition to relieving back pain, the stretching and exercise will pay off tremendously in labour and delivery and during those first days after the birth of your baby when your body is remembering how it 'normally' is. A few safe and gentle yoga stretches are offered below for you to try. If possible do each pose twice and hold for 4-5 deep breaths

Squatting Stretch (Malasana)

This is just what it sounds like. Balance your body; steady yourself with a counter, table, or piece of furniture and squat for one minute at a time (flat-footed if possible or with a book or folded blanket under your heels for support), 10 times a day. This is a great stretch and toner for legs and perineal muscles and a must for any woman planning to squat during second stage (the most efficient and natural position for birthing). Preparing for squatting is very important as it is physically demanding for western women who don't practice this position on a day-to-day basis.

Cobbler Sitting (Baddha Konasana)

Sit on the floor with knees bent and soles of the feet together (with knees out to the side like butterfly wings). Spend up to 10 breaths in this position. If your groin feels tight and uncomfortable in this position place a cushion or rolled up blanket under each knee for support until the groin stretches a little more. Baddha Konasana gives the inner thighs a good stretch and takes pressure off the lower back. For more support sit up against a wall to ensure your back is straight.

Pelvic Tilt

Lying on your back with knees bent and feet flat on the floor OR, if more than 20 weeks, stand against a wall with feet shoulder width apart. Exhale while pressing the small of your back against the floor or wall and tilting the lower pelvic area up or out away from the wall, then inhale and relax the spine. Repeat this several times. The standing position is best used after the fourth month of pregnancy.

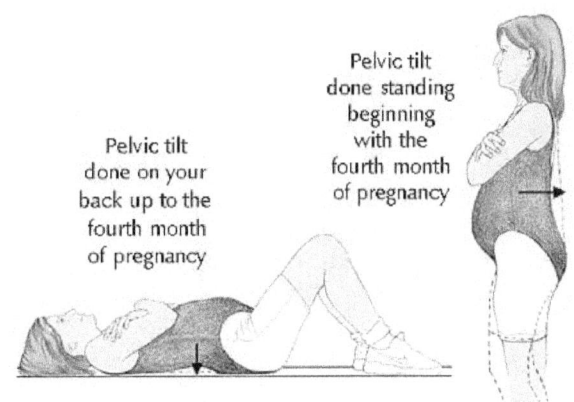

Pelvic tilt done on your back up to the fourth month of pregnancy

Pelvic tilt done standing beginning with the fourth month of pregnancy

Cat Stretch (Marjariasana)

You will feel new awareness and energy come to your spine after practicing this pose. The internal organs are also given renewed blood flow, helping to improve their action.

1. Come onto the floor on your hands and knees. Bring your hands directly under your shoulders with the tallest finger at 12'0'clock and your knees hips width apart. Become aware of the length and quality of the breath. Inhale to prepare.
2. Exhale slowly and completely as you begin to arch the back upward. Tuck the tailbone and the crown of the head moving them towards each other. Use your hands and knees for support

in the pose, keeping your arms long and pushing up away from the floor. Try to feel every part of the back, every vertebrae.

3. Inhale slowly and completely. Open the chest forward, lifting the heart centre, arching the back downward. Feel the tailbone and the crown of the head lifting equally towards the sky. Try to feel every part of the back, every vertebra.
4. Continue to coordinate the breath and the movement of the spine, repeating this sequence and many times as is desirable. When you are ready to stop simply bring the spine back to a neutral position, parallel to the floor.

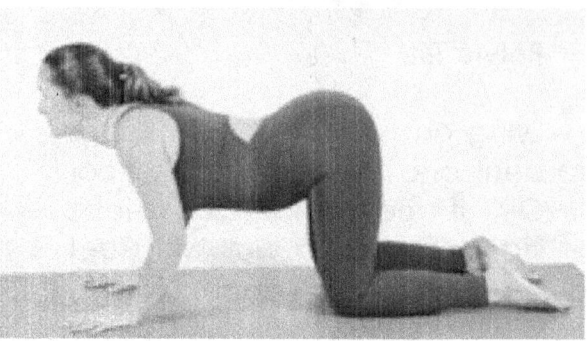

Benefits:

- Excellent for creating a supple spine, preventing injury
- Purifies the blood
- Reinvigorates the spine and internal organs
- Relieves tension in the low back

Modifications/Cautionary Notes:

- Maintain awareness of your back and neck. Do not over extend.
- Use the hands and knees for support without using them to push yourself more deeply into the arch. The body will naturally open with time.

- It may be beneficial to rest in Child's Pose (see variation in pic with head supported, knees apart and arms stretched forward) after ending the sequence (3-5 repetitions of cat/cow is enough).

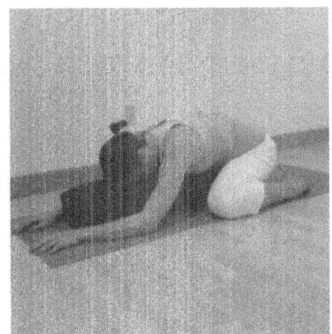

Spending time on all fours is also excellent for mums with a baby in the posterior position (facing forwards with their spine against yours when they should ideally be facing towards the back of your body). This position helps to encourage your baby to turn around the right way to make birthing easier and more comfortable, and don't lose hope, using this position, babies might even turn during labour (or at the very least it will take some of the pressure off your back).

Along with these stretches, moderate exercise is important. Review your exercise plan with your doctor or midwife before you begin. Pregnancy isn't the time to try to lose weight or begin a vigorous exercise routine but you can pursue exercise at a mild to moderate level and receive tremendous benefits from it.

The safest and most comfortable exercises for expectant mothers are:

- **Walking** it's easy and everyone can do it and it's the perfect way to get started if you didn't exercise before pregnancy
- Low impact aerobic classes, pilates or pregnancy exercise videotapes done at home.
- **Yoga**, great for stretching and opening the body, most studios have special classes for women who are pregnant (pregnancy or antenatal yoga).
- **Swimming**; it uses many different muscle groups and puts less gravitational strain on the joints (the water supports your weight, which is a welcomed relief for most and it helps you to practice slow rhythmical breathing).

Remember, the key to exercising during pregnancy is moderation. Don't go for the burn and don't exercise to exhaustion. A good rule of thumb is to slow down if you can't comfortably carry on a conversation while moving.

> *Unless you have a medical condition that restricts exercise, mild to moderate exercise is very safe during pregnancy. It's good for you as long as you don't overdo it and heed your body's warning signs such as: dizziness; feeling faint; contractions; difficulty walking; excessive fatigue; shortness of breath; vaginal bleeding; nausea; marked decrease in movement of your baby; intense pain anywhere, but especially your lower back or pelvic region.*
>
> *If you develop any of the above symptoms during or after exercising, stop immediately and call your hospital, doctor or midwife.*

PELVIC FLOOR MUSCLE EXERCISES

What are the pelvic floor muscles?

The floor of the pelvis is made up of layers of muscle and other tissues. These layers stretch like a hammock from the tailbone at the back to the pubic bone in front. A woman's pelvic floor supports the bladder, the womb (uterus) and the bowel. The urethra (front passage), the vagina (birth canal) and the rectum (back passage) pass through the pelvic floor muscles. The pelvic floor muscles play an important role in bladder and bowel control and sexual sensation.

The pelvic floor muscles can be weakened by:
- pregnancy and childbirth;
- continual straining to empty your bowels (constipation);
- persistent heavy lifting;
- a chronic cough (such as smoker's cough or chronic bronchitis and asthma);
- being quite overweight;
- changes in hormone levels at menopause (change of life); and
- lack of general fitness.

The benefits of pelvic floor exercises:

It is important for women of all ages to maintain pelvic floor muscle strength. Women with stress incontinence, that is, those who regularly lose urine when coughing, sneezing or exercising, should especially benefit from these exercises. **For pregnant women these exercises help the body to cope with the increasing weight of the baby. Healthy, fit muscles pre-natal will recover more readily after the birth.**

How to contract (and exercise) the pelvic floor muscles

The first thing to do is to correctly identify the muscles that need to be exercised.
Sit or lie down comfortably with the muscles of your thighs, buttocks and abdomen relaxed
Tighten the ring of muscle around the back passage as if you are trying to control diarrhea or wind. Relax it. Practice this movement several times until you are sure you are exercising the correct muscle. Try not to squeeze your buttocks.

When you are passing urine, try to stop the flow mid-stream, then restart it. Only do this to learn which muscles are the correct ones to use and then do it no more than once a week to cheek your progress, as this may interfere with normal bladder emptying.

NOTE: If you are unable to feel a definite squeeze and lift action of your pelvic floor muscles or are unable to even slow the stream of urine as described in point 3, you should seek professional help to get your pelvic floor muscles working correctly. Even women with very weak pelvic floor muscles can be taught these exercises by a physiotherapist or continence advisor with expertise in this area.

Doing pelvic floor exercises

Tighten and draw in around the anus, the vagina and the urethra all at once, lifting them UP inside. Try and hold this contraction strongly as you count to five then release and relax. You should have a definite feeling of 'letting go'.
Repeat ('squeeze and lift') and relax. It is important to rest for about 10 seconds in between each contraction. If you find it easy to hold for a count of five, try to hold for longer - up to ten seconds.
Repeat this as many times as you are able up to a maximum of 8-10 squeezes.
Now do five to ten short, fast, but strong contractions.
Do this whole exercise routine at least 4-5 times every day.

DO NOT hold your breath.
DO NOT push down instead of squeezing and lifting up.
DO NOT tighten your tummy, buttocks or thighs.

Do your exercises well - the quality is important. Fewer good exercises will be more beneficial than many half hearted ones.
DO NOT overdo these exercises, an overly tightened pelvic floor can lead to the need for an episiotomy (a cut made to the skin between the vaginal opening and the anus to widen the opening to allow the baby's head to pass through).

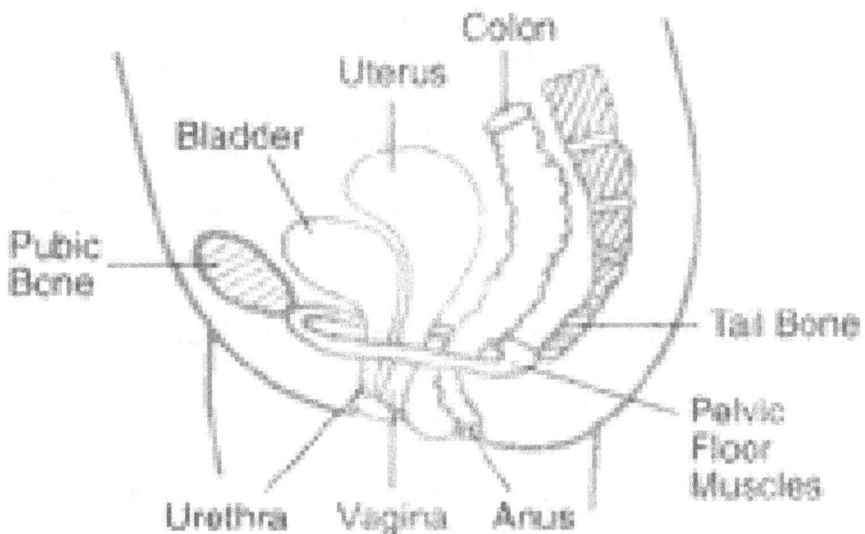

Partners:

Don't be fooled into thinking this is women's business! Men need strong pelvic floor muscles too in order to avoid incontinence in later life...

PERINEAL MASSAGE

Perineal Massage is one of the oldest and surest ways of improving the health, blood flow, elasticity, and relaxation of the pelvic floor muscles. Practiced during the last 4-8 weeks of pregnancy, this technique improves the chances of birthing your baby without tearing or an episiotomy. **If you want to avoid tearing or an episiotomy the importance of this massage cannot be overemphasized – particularly for first time mums and mums who have not previously birthed vaginally.**

When your perineal rim is soft and relaxed, your baby easily slips past the rim and out of the vagina. It is far more effective for you to stretch these tissues beforehand than have a midwife or doctor do it while your baby's head is crowning (just about to come out from inside the vagina). Taking the time to do to this massage will pay off. It is simple and yet so very effective.

Massaging with oil helps to stretch the perineal muscles and soften the tissue, both of which will reduce resistance against your baby's head. As you or your partner do the massage, you can learn to identify which muscles you will need to relax for birthing; and you can teach these muscles to relax and open outward in response to pressure.

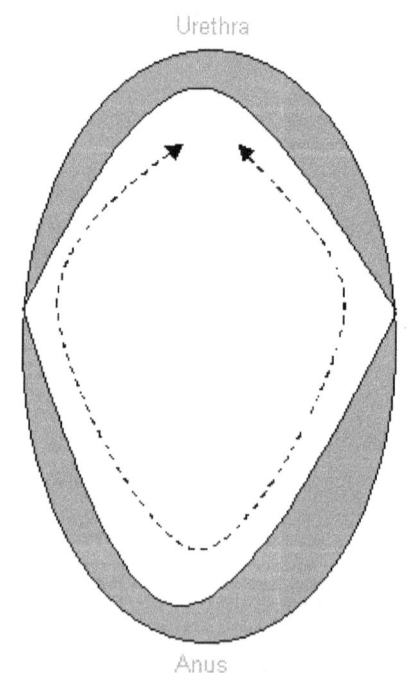

The massage should be done **every day for around five minutes**, beginning about four to eight weeks before your estimated due date. Because of your increased size and the awkwardness of bending around your abdomen, it may be easier to have someone else do the massage for you. If you are doing the massage by yourself you'll find it easier if you place one foot on the seat of a chair or the toilet. This allows you to work around and under your belly.

Be sure that fingernails are smooth and short when doing the massage. A disposable rubber glove will ensure that there are no rough surfaces to irritate the vaginal tissue. You may use virgin olive oil, sweet almond oil or a lubricating gel. <u>Avoid</u> perfumed oils and petroleum-based products (i.e. do <u>not</u> use baby oil or Vaseline).

Technique: Pour a little of the oil (sweet almond or jojoba are best) into a shallow bowl, around 10mls should be ample. Be sure to discard oil that is left after massaging. Alternately, use an organic, water-based lubricant such as Yes.

Stand with one leg up on the toilet or sit with your back resting against pillows and get comfortable. It's a good idea to use a mirror during the first few times that you do this exercise. It will assist you in identifying the muscles that are involved and will allow you to observe the stretching at the edge of the perineum. Alternately, if you have been practicing your squats, squatting in the shower is also a good position for this massage.

Dip your thumbs into the oil up to the first knuckle to thoroughly moisten. If a partner is doing the massage, they will use both their first and second fingers, dipped in oil to the second knuckle and inserted into the vagina approximately 3-5cm, pressing downward on the area between the vagina and the anus. Rub the oil into the inner edge of the perineum and the, lower vaginal wall.

Maintaining a steady pressure, slide the fingers upward along the sides of the vagina in a 'U', sling-type motion. This pressure will stretch the tissue. The muscles surrounding the vaginal opening, as well as the outer rim of the perineum. Be sure to stretch the inner area as well as the outer rim. You may feel tightness in the muscles to begin with, but with a little practice, the tissue will relax easily.

Preparation: This whole technique is about preparation. Use the massage for the final 4-8 weeks of your pregnancy to help prepare the area for the stretching that will occur as your baby's head passes through. This practice will be *oh so worth it* when you get to that moment of birth with no need for an episiotomy.

Practice relaxing the extended muscles by picturing the perineum opening outwards as pressure is applied. The opening rosebud or lotus flower is a good visualisation to accompany the perineal massage, use your relaxation breath to help you ease into the sensation. Pick a time in your day to practice the massage, during, just before or after a shower is a good time.

Work: Your doctor or midwife might use the perineal massage technique to help your body stretch and ease the perineum around your baby's head as it passes through the vaginal opening. But all you have to do is breathe and work with your body and know what a great job you have done in preparing your mind and your body for this moment.

> **Partners:** Your midwife might suggest to your partner to pant or hold back her breathing just as your baby's head is coming out. This is so that your baby doesn't come out too quickly, before mum's body has had a chance to stretch fully around your baby's head. By helping her to hold the energy in with a few shallow breaths, you will be helping her to have a more comfortable birth and to avoid any tearing. Once baby's head is out, she will be able to 'push' and breathe fully again.

Even if you don't like the idea of practicing the perineal massage everyday for a month or so I urge you to at least give it one or two go's just to help prepare yourself for the sensation of the stretch. It is a burning kind of feeling, just like if you stretch out the edges of your mouth too far and your lips start to pull. At least if you have tried this on your perineum you wont be startled or shocked as your baby's head passes through (the sensation eases very quickly as the perineum becomes numb with the stretch) and you will be able to relax into the stretch to make it even quicker and easier.

DISTRACTION PRACTICE

Very Important: You need to prepare for distractions during your labour and birthing, these might come in the form of blood pressure readings, monitoring baby's heartbeat, movement from home to the hospital or conversations that need to be had.

Prepare for these distractions by building them into your relaxation practice:
- Ask your partner to come in and pretend to take your blood pressure during a relaxation session. **Partner:** give her 5-10 minutes to become deeply relaxed and then go up to her and place your hand on her arm at about the same place that a midwife will place the blood pressure cuff during labour. Hold your hand there and say something about the midwife taking her blood pressure reading or tell her what a wonderful job she is doing to prepare for the birth of your child. After a minute or two, leave her to finish her relaxation session.
- Practice the rapid relaxation technique in a busy place – on a bus, at work, or in your doctor's waiting room.
- Practice your relaxation in different positions and in different rooms of your house so you don't become limited in where and when you feel deeply relaxed.

Preparing your mind and body for the work it will do on the day that your baby will be born is an important part of a good pregnancy. Hopefully, by the time you get to this part of the book you are **aware** of how this preparation will be helpful during labour and the benefits of using the techniques during pregnancy.

With practice I am sure you will be noticing how easy it is to begin to **trust** that the techniques are useful in labour and that your body will respond quickly and easily.

And now that you have the techniques you need to **work** with your body you might be starting to realise that you have already made some very important **choices** with regard to the type of birth experience you and your baby are going to have.

Remember that you also have choices with regard to how to use the techniques outlined in this book. You or your partner can modify any of the scripts or techniques to suit yourselves. Some of the wording in the affirmations or scripts might see a bit cheesy or wishy washy to you – change them. There's no point in having your partner say something they are not comfortable saying, both of you need to be as calm and comfortable as possible.

You can also choose to leave out any of the techniques that don't suit you – none of them are make or break – although I would urge you to find some sort of method for achieving physical relaxation and think about using your breath in some way.

#3 Checking in – Self-Awareness Exercise.

Thinking about labour and birthing, on a scale from 0 to 100, where 0 represents not at all and 100 means completely, how would you rate yourself <u>right now</u> in terms of:

0   100
___

CONFIDENCE

0   100
___

CALMNESS

Place a mark on the lines above to indicate how you feel <u>right now</u>

Thinking about labour and birthing, on a scale from 0 to 100, where 0 represents not at all and 100 means completely, how would you <u>want to feel during labour and birthing</u> in terms of:

0   100
___

CONFIDENCE

0   100
___

CALMNESS

Place a mark on the lines above to indicate how you <u>want to feel during labour and birthing</u>

Has there been any change since you last rated yourself?

CHAPTER 4 CHOICES

There are many choices that can be made with regard to birthing, many are about preference, some are more crucial to the health and well-being of mum and bub.

It is very important that you discuss any pre-considered choices with your doctor or midwife. They may have policies or legal considerations to abide by or be aware of extra information or research findings that could affect your decisions. This person is someone you have chosen to trust during your pregnancy and birthing so use their knowledge and expertise to guide you in making the choices that are right for you and your baby.

Here is some very general information about some of the choices you might like to think about for your baby's birthing. Keep in mind that your end goal is always **healthy mum, healthy baby**. It is also good to remember that you have already made some very important choices, which have set you up for a welcoming birthing experience.

You Have Already Chosen:

- to prepare for a natural birth,
- to focus on welcoming your child,
- to have a well informed and supportive partner,
- to go into labour and birth with a calm and positive attitude, and
- to make choices that are right for you and your baby at the time.

Sometimes decisions need to be made during labour, some of which can come as a surprise, this may trigger the flight or fight response – use an affirmation or the Rapid relaxation technique to re-establish your relaxation if this happens. Further, by understanding the choices you have there will be less chance of surprise and you will feel more calm and in control, regardless of the situation.

Some women prefer to wear their own clothing during labour. Others prefer the hospital gowns because they are loose and can be soiled, discarded and replaced with ease. Many women find that any clothing at all is a nuisance and naked is best.

BIRTH CHOICES

Despite birth involving quite a large number of factors that contribute to the way things go, you can still be informed about the possibilities and learn which are more likely to occur. You can then decide what is ideal and what you will focus on, what techniques and choices are going to help you create the environment for the birth you are wanting and the welcome you would like to give your baby.

The use of any procedure is the decision of the patient. Hospital staff may refer to them as hospital policy and consider them mandatory (most likely with good reason); nevertheless, the labouring woman may refuse any of them. As with all items of choice, each woman should consider the reasons for each of these and discuss your preferences with your obstetrician or midwife. You are at all times in control of your body and your baby, you must give consent to any medical intervention; but, always remember your end goal - **healthy mum, healthy baby**.

Things to consider in decision making :

- why you have made this choice,

- how this choice is helping in your birthing preparations, and

- how this choice will help you have the birthing you are preparing for.

Birth Choices

This is not an exhaustive list of your choices but it might help you to get started with thinking about how you would like to work through your labour and all of the choices you have available to you:

Your Care Provider

- Obstetrician
- GP/midwife shared care
- Midwife

Location of Birth

- Home
- Birthing Centre
- Hospital

Testing, IVs and Monitoring

- Intermittent fetal monitoring v constant monitoring
- IV in non-dominant hand with freedom to move around (if necessary)
- Blood pressure readings
- 4 hourly internal examinations v only when medically necessary

Pain Management

- Self-Hypnosis
- Massage
- Breathing
- Physical relaxation
- Meditation
- Visualisation
- Water
- TENS (Transcutaneous Electrical Nerve Stimulation) machine
- Epidural
- Gas/O_2
- Narcotics

Other natural techniques

- Acupressure
- Acupuncture
- Herbal Tea

> Eating and drinking during labour can be very important, particularly if labour is long. Fatigue can cause labour to slow and the labouring woman to give up. Regular nourishment prevents this.

- Aromatherapy

Clothing, Eating and Drinking

- Own clothes
- Hospital gown
- No clothing
- Hospital meals

- Own snacks
- Water
- Fruit Juice
- Sports drinks
- Ice chips

Who is in Attendance?

- Baby's father
- Sister, mother, close friend
- Doula*
- Independent midwife
- Baby's older siblings

Second Stage

- Spontaneous Pushing v waiting to be told to push**
- Episiotomy v possible tearing
- Active management of third stage (using Syntocinon) v spontaneous expulsion of placenta

Induction methods (might be offered to get labour started or if labour seemingly pauses during the process.)

- Sexual intercourse (if you are able to be at home!)
- Homeopathy
- Acupuncture
- Reflexology
- Relaxation and visualisation
- Bowel irritation (e.g. hot & spicy foods, an enema)
- Prostaglandin gel (try sex first! **This hormone is also present in the male ejaculation/semen)**
- Artificial rupture of membranes
- Using an anmicot (glove with a hook attached to one finger - suggested choice if required)
- Using an amniotomy hook
- Syntocinon (synthetic oxytocin)
- None

Checking Baby

- Immediate skin-to-skin contact between mother and baby
- Delayed weighing and other newborn tests
- Vitamin K Shot ***
- Circumcision
- Immunisation/Vaccination

Other Post-Partum Choices

- When to cut the cord (if at all)
- What to do with the placenta (if anything)
- Cord-blood collection or donation

*Doulas are people (usually women) educated in pregnancy, birth and post-natal issues (such as breastfeeding) who provide informational, emotional and physical support throughout pregnancy, labour, childbirth and the early postpartum period.

**Once the cervix has dilated to around10 centimetres, many women begin to feel an urge to push. Some women feel this urge before they are completely open and occasionally women don't get the urge at all. In this case if your surges are still coming on regularly, working with your surge is still very effective.

***The vitamin K shot is given to aid in blood clotting. There is vitamin K present in the colostrum, which is the sticky fluid that appears before your breast milk comes in.

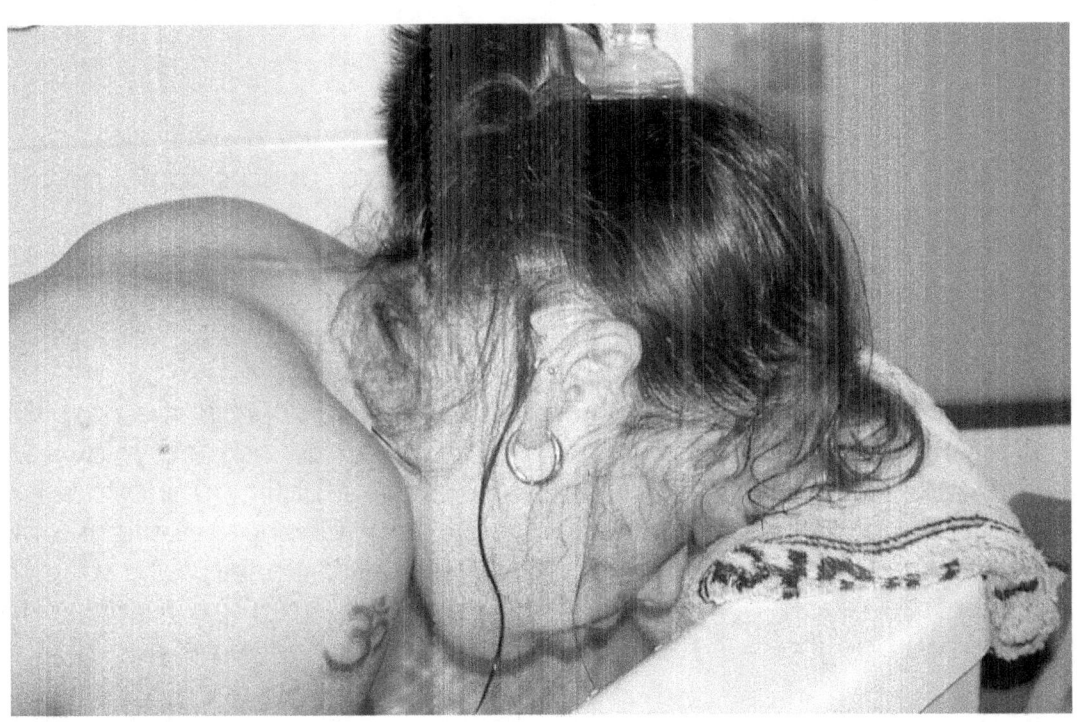

CHOOSING A COMFORTABLE POSITION FOR EFFICIENT LABOUR AND BIRTHING

Try the positions together with massage or in the shower or bath to maximise your level of comfort. Use the bed, fitball, your partner, your midwife or anything else in the room for support and to find the position that is right for you (this is not necessarily the same position that best suits your Dr or other well meaning person).

Here are some suggestions for positions you may find useful during labour. Trust your instincts on the day and do whatever feels right and comfortable for you. Your midwife may offer good suggestions, listen to the suggestions and decide for yourself if you would like to accept the advice.

Basics to remember with all of these suggestions:

- You should be as fully supported as possible, using people, pillows, beanbags or furniture, so you can fully relax.
- Knees should be bent to avoid tiredness in the legs and to make pelvic rocking easier if desired.
- Your feet should be apart to give a wide base for support, and to encourage opening within the body.
- Be creative in your adaptation of available furniture in the hospital. If you need extra pillows a birthing stool or chair, ask your midwife.
- Once a comfortable position is found, use it until you find that it is no longer helping you in your relaxation. Change positions only when you feel the need to, unless you are positioning for a specific purpose, such as to help the baby turn from posterior or to encourage the baby to move down further into the pelvis.

Principles of good labour and birthing positions:

- The first stage is all about feeling comfortable, move around until you find a position in which you are able to focus solely on your breathing, relaxation or visualization.
- During transition you may become restless and want to move from your previously perfect position, just follow your body's lead it will guide you into a good position for birthing.
- An upright, forward, open pelvis, knees close to chest type position is ideal for second stage, however if you are feeling unsure, your midwife will be the best person to listen to and will help you into the position that is right for you and your baby.

First stage

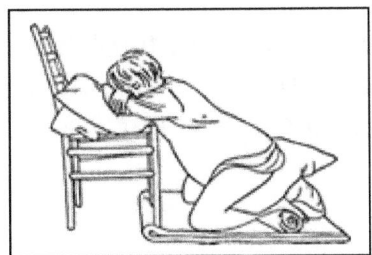

Leaning forward with pillows under your bottom, behind your knees and under your feet is one of the most comfortable positions for labour for many women. You can use this position in the shower over a plastic chair or fit ball (with a mat under your knees), over the side of the bath or with the back of the bed raised you can use a position similar to 'child's' pose' from yoga (see earlier section on preparing your body).

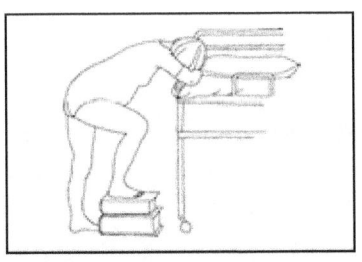

Some women find asymmetrical positions help ease pressure points (try this if you are experiencing sciatica).

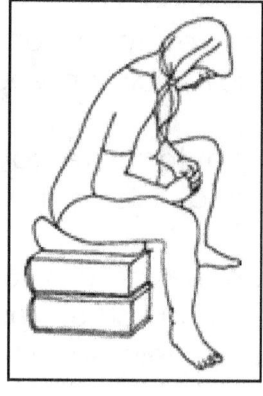

You can easily use a bedpan like this, however, most women find a birthing stool more comfortable, it also offers better positioning (or the toilet). A fit ball is probably the best way to achieve this position, or the edge of the bed or bath might also work for you.

Transition

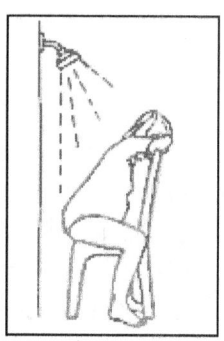

Standing or sitting in the shower offers natural relief from any discomfort and gives you a nice feeling to focus on, especially towards the end of the first stage.

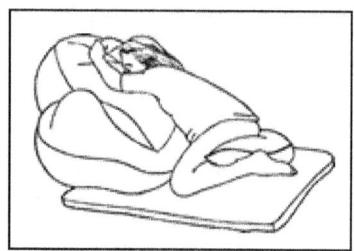

It is easy to rest and relax fully between surges if you are well supported by pillows or a beanbag.

Use a heat pack or well wrung-out hot, wet towels draped over the buttocks for lower back pressure or discomfort if baby is posterior. You can also combine this pressure from a strong massage down on to the sacrum.

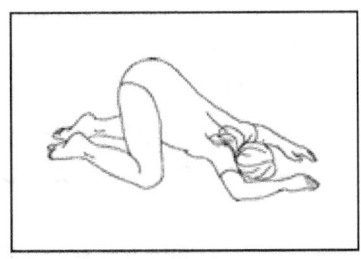
Use the knee-chest or polar bear position to help work through a premature urge to push during transition, this position also helps to turn a baby that is posterior. Work with your body, listen to your body, it will know when it is time to bare down. If you listen to your body and don't push aggressively, don't hold your breath or use overt force there will be no premature urge to push and no danger of injuring your cervix. Just breathe your baby down, let your body birth your baby.

Second stage

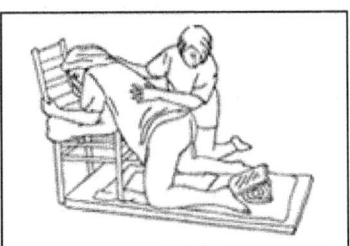
During the second stage, you will need to be well supported so you can focus on working with your surges effectively. Some women seek something to grip and many prefer to be upright with feet planted firmly on the floor, whatever position you are in, continue to breathe deeply and keep your body as loose, limp and relaxed as possible. Use your partner, midwife or furniture/props for support.

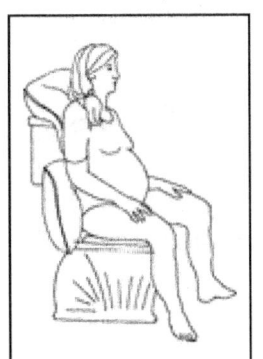
Sitting on the toilet can help you to identify the area to bear down into, as your surges become more coordinated with your breath they will be more effective. This might also be achieved on a birthing stool. A mirror is useful to enable you, your partner and your midwife to see the baby's progress.

A supported squatting position can help to open your pelvis and uses gravity to assist the baby's movement down. If you get tired in this position it is very easy to lean forward onto your hands for support into the all-fours position, which is a great second stage position.

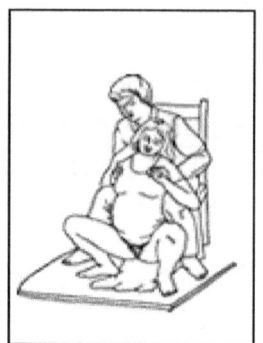

Standing or leaning forward during the second stage will help your pelvis to open fully and allow your coccyx (tailbone) to open a further 1½-2 cm to allow your baby's head to pass through your pelvis. Squatting or bringing your knees up to your chest can also shorten the path between your cervix and the perineum. If you choose to lay, try laying on your side so the tailbone still has movement, you can also sit up during your surges, knees apart and bent, chest right over towards the bed and sitting forward off your tailbone. Your partner and midwife will support your feet, or if the end of the bed drops down you can squat over the end of the bed. If you are in this position and your baby's head rests on the perineum for longer than you would like (crowning) try turning over on to all fours or get into a forward squatting position so that baby's head can move under rather than over (or through if it tears) the perineum.

Leaning forward over pillows or a beanbag is useful if you want to be on the bed.

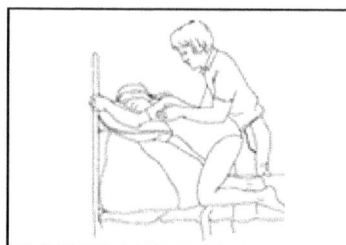

Basic Principles:

- **First stage is all about being comfortable; any position that helps you to manage the surges is a good one!**
- **Second stage is all about helping your baby down and out, open your body, lean forward and work with your surges**

THE USE OF WATER FOR LABOUR AND/OR BIRTH

Many women notice a huge change in the way they are managing the sensations of labour once they get into the bath or shower. Whether it is your focus on the feel of the water on your skin or the level of relaxation you are able to achieve in the bath, the use of water is undoubtedly one of the number one natural methods for managing discomfort during labour.

The benefits of water immersion, or hydrotherapy, in labour have been studied and assessed by many experienced midwives, researchers and doctors all over the world. It is clear from common findings that including a pool of warm water in the birthing room, adds a whole new dimension to the experience of childbirth. A recent study of 1,300 water births found that the use of a birth pool is rated very highly by women, whether having their first or subsequent baby and their enthusiasm is shared by midwives (Odent, 1983).

Common findings are that being in the bath during labour or using a birth pool:

- Increases privacy,
- Provides significant relief from discomfort,
- Reduces the need for medical intervention and pain medication,
- Facilitates a woman's sense of control in labour,
- Enables the woman to easily change positions,
- Encourages a more efficient and therefore faster labour,
- Promotes relaxation and prevents fatigue,
- Helps to reduce tears and the need for episiotomy,
- Is highly recommended by mothers who have used one, and
- Encourages an easier birth for the mother and a gentler welcome for the baby.

Your choices for the use of water during labour and/or birthing include:

- Bath
- Shower
- Spa
- Labour in water
- Labour and Birth in water
- Birth in Water

There is a lot of research regarding water births, which can easily be found on the internet. When you are reading about the relative benefits of water birth for mother and baby, it is worth distinguishing between the use of water during labour and an actual water birth. Talk to your doctor or midwife about the pros and cons and be aware that some hospitals don't officially allow water births due to perceived risks and associated legal implications.

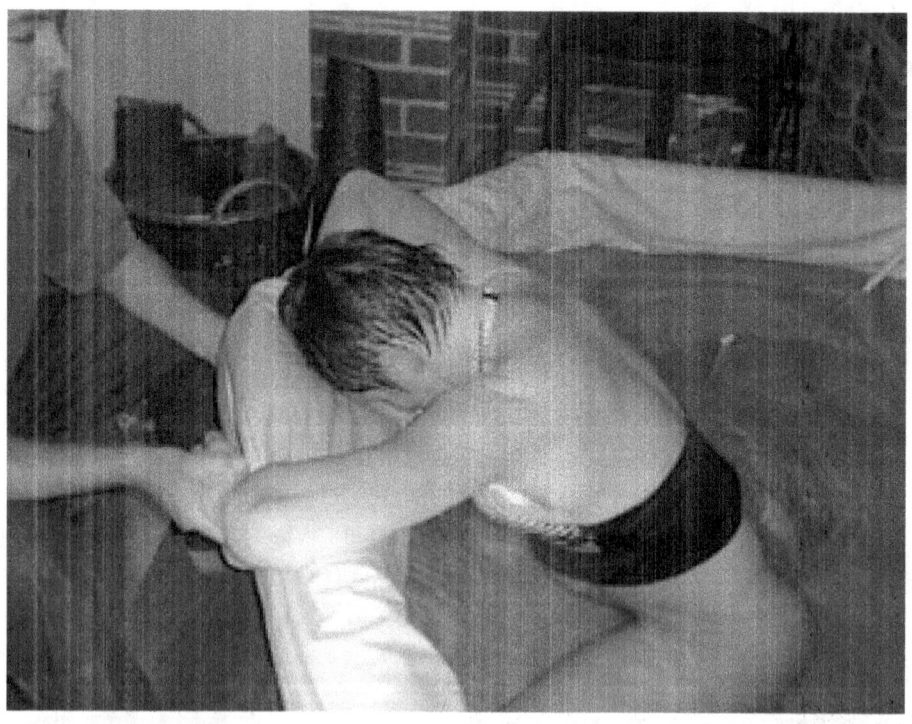

ESTIMATED DUE DATE - EDD

A baby's gestation is 40 weeks, 280 days or 10 lunar months. Modern science tells us that it can be anywhere from 265 days to 300 days or 37 weeks to 42 weeks. So the due date really is an estimation because a lot depends on menstrual cycles. Do not be overly worried if you go beyond the estimated due date or if you start to go into labour the week before because you are still within that window period.

Often if you go over the estimate date well meaning relatives and friends start to put pressure on you and you start to feel a little anxious. The doctor may also say that he may need to see you a little more frequently in a tone that you may pick up that something is not quite right. This in turn may create tension within you so practicing your relaxation and remaining calm is very important. Keep focused on the birthing you want. If there is a complication, be calm and take your time to make any decisions that are needed.

There are times when a medical induction is necessary, for example if the pregnant woman's blood pressure has become high or if they have developed gestational diabetes. The relaxation techniques will help you through whatever turn your birthing takes – use them! A calm and confident mum will have a much better experience no matter what type of birthing is taking place, as opposed to one who is anxious and frightened.

> ### Signals That Require Your Attention – Special Circumstances
>
> Contact your doctor or midwife regarding anything that seems unusual to you, particularly if you experience any of the following:
>
> - Any vaginal loss, excessive vomiting or diarrhea.
> - If you don't feel your baby move over a period of 12 hours or even less than that if you just become aware of it - ring your hospital or doctor. Often you only need the reassurance that everything is OK.
> - If you have been attending your doctor regularly and suddenly your blood pressure goes up then they may ask you to attend a little more often.
> - If you start to get headaches or spots in front of your eyes then don't hesitate to call them.
> - Any sudden gushes of fluid as if the membranes had released.
> - DO NOT HESITATE to call '000' if you feel that something is wrong with you or your baby.

BRAXTON HICKS SURGES

As you move towards your birth experience the Braxton Hicks waves might become more apparent. These are great opportunities to practice your controlled breathing. When you recognise the tightening you can take some of those deep slow breaths and encourage the breathing to become more natural.

Lightening/Dropping (the change in the shape of your belly when your baby's head is fully engaged)

Lightening (not the word I would have chosen to describe the feelings associated with your baby moving further down into your pelvis!) is often a sign that your birthing day is getting closer, though it may still be a few weeks off. For some first time mums babies don't fully engage and therefore the 'drop' or 'lightening' is not experienced. This also means that if your membranes release during labour there might be a gush of fluid as your baby's head wont be blocking the cervix. It is not a problem if your baby doesn't engage fully during your pregnancy, it will happen during labour. If lightening does occur you might find that you now have more room to breathe, however, sitting becomes a whole new experience! Your tailbone becomes quite prominent and you may find your legs want to splay out to the side a little more. Some women describe a feeling as if everything between their legs is going to fall out! Try to avoid the pregnancy waddle of throwing the abdomen forward and walking with your feet turned out, this places excessive strain on your back. If your baby has dropped you might feel a sensation of pressure down low and your belly might sit a little lower than before.

The 'Show'

The show is a glob (very technical term meaning jelly like blob J) of mucous released from the cervix as it begins to thin and open (sometimes referred to as ripening of the cervix). This glob has acted as a plug for your uterus during your pregnancy, sealing it and preventing any external bacteria or foreign bodies getting in. Some women notice a small amount of blood released with the mucous plug while others report that it was just a clear/yellowish glob. The show can occur weeks before you go into labour, at the onset of labour or during labour. It just depends when your cervix softens and opens enough for the plug to be released and fall out. Also, the plug can come out all at once or a bit at a time over a few days, again, it depends on your body, how much prostaglandin is being produced (or offered by your partner!) and how open your cervix is.

Leaking

Occasionally there may be a leaking of amniotic fluid causing you to think that your membranes have released. Unless there is a large gush of fluid then there is nothing to be concerned about, notify your health care provider but do not be too concerned. The amniotic fluid replenishes itself completely every three hours or so. Your baby will not be harmed and if there is a slight tear or rip in your membranes, they will also repair themselves in a relatively short time. It may be a little embarrassing or annoying if you are leaking fluid and don't have a pad available, so around the 36 week mark, pack one in your handbag or glove-box just in case! Definitely do not use a tampon. If there is a flow or gush of fluid, an odour or discolouration, contact your doctor immediately.

Premature rupturing of membranes

Premature rupture of membranes involves your membranes releasing without your surges beginning – i.e. when the release is not followed by the onset of labour. If you do not go into spontaneous labour within 12 hours of your membranes releasing, infection becomes a real risk as the seal between the inside of your body, your baby and the outside world has been broken. With a course of antibiotics, there are doctors who will allow a woman to go 2 or 3 days before medically inducing labour. Most doctors will want to induce after 6 or 12 hours. This is the time when you should ask whether there is a medical emergency. Is there already an infection or other problem? If you would rather wait a little longer ask if they can keep a close eye on it rather than start labour, weigh up the associated risks and make an informed decision.

INDUCING LABOUR – Medical v. alternative induction methods

Medical Induction Methods:

Prostaglandin Gel

If you have gone beyond your due date or have had some problem arise during your pregnancy (e.g. high blood pressure) your doctor might suggest that your labour be induced. If your cervix has not yet softened or begun to open a gel containing the prostaglandin hormone will be placed on your cervix to begin this process (to 'ripen' your cervix). For some women the gel works overnight and labour continues naturally from there, others need to continue with the process of medical induction. For a few women 3 or more applications of the gel are required to soften the cervix, this can mean you are in hospital for 1-2 full days before going into labour. Prostaglandin is naturally available in the male ejaculation so to avoid the gel, enjoy a good love making session with your partner! Stay lying down for 20 minutes after sex so that the prostaglandins have time to act on the cervix (see the next section for more information about this).

Syntocinon

Once your cervix has softened and begun to open either naturally or from the use of the gel, if your labour needs to be induced, your doctor will attach an intravenous supply of Syntocinon, usually in the back of your hand. Syntocinon is the synthetic version of the hormone oxytocin, the hormone that stimulates your uterus and creates the surges. Oxytocin is produced naturally in the female body when labour begins spontaneously but also during sex if orgasm is reached and when the nipples or clitoris are being stimulated. So, *good* sex is the best method of achieving a natural onset of labour and avoiding medical induction – you need the male and female orgasm to get the most from this method. If you do need the Syntocinon drip during your labour you will still be able to move around, get in the shower or bath and practice all of your relaxation techniques. Your labour will still be a wonderful process towards welcoming your baby and with the right doctor managing the process the surges brought on by the Syntocinon will be very similar in intensity and rate as surges brought on by naturally occurring oxytocin (communication with your Dr is the key here – talk to them about easing into labour rather than just 'turning it on').

Artificial rupturing of the membranes

Artificial rupturing of the membrane is the third means of initiating labour medically. While some women find no difference in the strength of the surge, others report that they experienced surges that were much more intense after the membrane had been ruptured. This is due to the differential pressure placed on your cervix by your baby's head. With the membrane intact the amniotic fluid helps to evenly distribute the pressure from your baby's head around the entire rim of your cervix. When the membranes have released it is more likely that there will be more pressure on one part of your cervix than another, this uneven pressure can create a more intense sensation for some women.

Maintaining your membrane intact can also facilitate the effectiveness of your surges by creating more leverage between your uterus and your baby's bottom. To help push bub down and out while protecting your baby from the direct pressure of your surging uterus. There's no reason why a baby cannot be born with the membranes still intact (midwives see this as a very special event when it occurs), however, most times if your membrane hasn't already released, it will break as your baby's head crowns, alleviating the burning stretch for you and creating a very easy and comfortable ride out for your baby.

Sometimes the doctor or midwife will want to release the membrane to check if the baby is okay. If it is suspected that the baby is in distress, breaking the membranes to see if there is meconium (baby's first poo) in the water can tell them if intervention is required to help your baby out quickly. If your doctor or midwife suspects that your baby is in distress start talking to them, ask what is happening and what they believe needs to be done? Then take a moment, a deep breath and let your partner help you make the choice that needs to be made. Your doctor or midwife can release the membrane in one of two ways: using an amniohook; or using an amnicot.

The amnicot is (was) my personal choice for this procedure as your doctor or midwife has more control over where the hook is placed when it is attached to the end of their finger. Although the amniohook is not a long instrument there is still the slightly increased risk of it grazing the cervix. Having said all of that, my personal choice, assuming labour is progressing normally, is to avoid (i.e. say 'no' to) an amniotomy altogether.

In this situation you might hear your doctor or midwife refer to an ARM (artificial rupture of membranes).

If you are using an obstetrician it is worth finding out if they routinely perform ARM or if they believe in spontaneous rupture.

Natural methods of bringing labour on...

Things to try at home if you are near or over your estimated due date:

- **Love-making (hugs before drugs).** Kissing, hugging, fondling, and gentle nipple or clitoral stimulation triggers the hormonal connection between the breast and vagina. Producing the natural oxytocin that can start uterine surges. If the stimulation of one nipple is not sufficient to start surges, try stimulation of both nipples simultaneously. Prolonged or vigorous nipple stimulation is not advised, not only can it make the nipples sore but can also have an adverse effect on the baby by creating hyperstimulation.
- **Sex.** If your membrane has not released, have sex. The male semen contains prostaglandin, a hormone that helps to soften the cervix. The female orgasm produces oxytocin, the hormone that carries the message for your uterus to surge. Nature has, indeed, a wonderful plan. That which puts the baby into the uterus can nicely assist in helping to bring it out.
- **Visualization.** While your nipples or clitoris are being stimulated, use an opening visualization, focusing on a rosebud or lotus flower slowly unfolding and opening. Gently direct your breath down into your vagina while visualizing.
- **Tea.** Try red raspberry leaf tea, 2-3 cups a day in the third trimester can help to tone the uterus (if your uterus is particularly sensitive to the tea drink it weak or only 1 cup a day or every second day).
- **Walk.** Walk, walk, and then walk some more but not to the extent that you become tired.
- **Bath.** If your membranes have not released, take a medium-hot bath. It helps if you or your partner scoops the water over your nipples and your abdomen. Use a few drops of lavender oil in the bath to make it even more relaxing.
- **Fear Release & relaxation.** Your **BirthSkills CD** or partner can take you through a fear release session, sometimes simply focusing on relaxing your body can help.
- **Acupressure or reflexology.** An experienced therapist can stimulate points in the body or feet to encourage the natural onset of labour.

- Acupuncture. Like acupressure, there are points that an acupuncturist is able to activate for the easy and effective induction of labour.
- **Primrose Oil**. Evening Primrose Oil capsules can assist in softening (ripening) the cervix. This can be applied directly to the cervix or taken orally, discuss with a health care practitioner.
- **Hot spicy foods**. The "beer and pizza" startup has more than occasional success, try Mexican, Asian or Italian food. [Beware – the reason this works so well is the same as the 'cleanse the bowel' method below.] Enjoy a glass of wine with your spicy meal. Since you are at the end of your pregnancy, your baby's development will not be at risk at this point – <u>one</u> glass of a mild alcoholic beverage (wine or beer are fine – but not spirits) may provide you with just the relaxation you need.
- **Cleanse the bowel**. Often the pulsating effect of emptying the bowel can stimulate the production of prostaglandin, the hormone that thins and softens the cervix. Also, the movement of the pulsating of the bowel next to the uterus can be enough to get the uterus pulsating too.

> *Prolapse of the umbilical cord (when the cord slips through the cervix before baby's body), is an emergency requiring immediate medical assistance. This is more likely in circumstances where membranes have released and the baby's head is not engaged (and therefore not blocking the cervix). It is also more common in vaginal breech births. If you are at home and suspect cord prolapse, put your head down and backside up and get an ambulance. If you need to, manually push the cord back up into the vagina.*

Using your physical relaxation techniques, go deeply into relaxation. Allow your entire body to let go…

Imagine talking with your baby, asking if she is ready to be born and be welcomed into your family…

Ask yourself if you are truly ready for this amazing journey to continue to the next stage…

Think about trust.

Have faith.

Imagine that you are consciously in control of your hormones and that you are able to turn on the flow of oxytocin in your body…feel it flowing down through your body, around your abdomen and into your cervix.

Your body is ready, your baby is ready, your mind is ready…

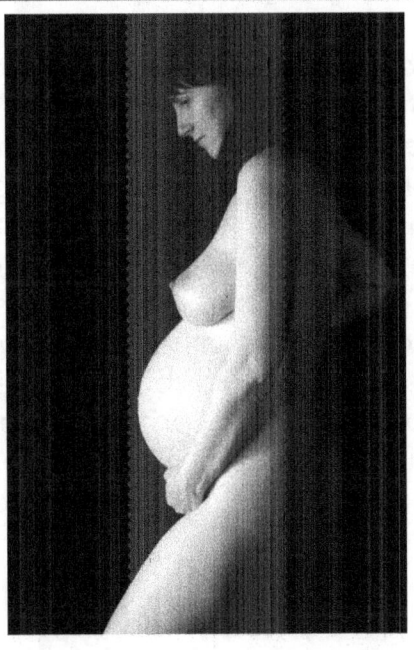

UNDERSTANDING MEDICAL PAIN MANAGEMENT

While analgesics and anesthetics are better and safer than ever, there is no perfect pain medication - one that works, yet is perfectly safe for mother and baby. By understanding what obstetrical drugs are available, what benefits and risks they carry, and how to use them wisely, you will best be able to decide which, if any, you want to use.

You may undertake extensive research about the use of medical pain relief, be fully prepared for the use of natural pain management techniques, and still decide during labour, with your partner, that it would be in the best interest of you and your baby and the progress of your labour to get some medical pain relief. Here are some suggestions about choosing the right form of medical pain relief during your labour:

- **Select the right drug.** With the assistance of your partner, discuss with your doctor, midwife or anesthesiologist which drug is best for your particular labour situation. Which one is likely to give you the quickest, most effective relief with minimal effects on your baby?
- **Select the right time.** Analgesics given too early can slow the progress of labour. In the early stages of labour, narcotics (including pethidine) are known to decrease the strength of surges and slow dilation of the cervix. If given too late, the effects on your baby will still be evident at birth.
- **Select the right route**. Getting the drug intravenously (directly into a vein, for example, on the back of your hand) gives you relief more quickly than an intramuscular injection. Intravenous drugs also wear off faster. After an intravenous injection a mother usually feels some relief within 5-10 minutes; this relief may last around an hour. Intramuscular injections, on the other hand, typically take half an hour to an hour to reach full effect, but the relief may last 3-4 hours. Most women choose the intravenous route; if labour pain is overwhelming enough to require medical relief, you want it to happen fast, and you might also need intravenous fluids.

Gas (Entonox)

The 'gas' available during labour is usually 50% nitrous oxide/50% oxygen (N_2O), and is otherwise known as laughing gas. It has been used since the late 1880's. N_2O is breathed into the lungs and very quickly enters the blood stream. N_2O reaches the brain within about 15-30 seconds. The amount of N_2O that reaches the brain varies, depending on the breath taken and correct use of the mask or mouthpiece.

The effectiveness of the gas as pain relief in labour varies from woman to woman. Most find that it does not entirely relieve the pain but produces enough of an analgesic effect to manage pain during an intense surge.

Known disadvantages of using the gas during labour include:

- Nausea and/or vomiting;
- Not a sure form of pain relief;
- Women can become drowsy, confused or disorientated. Some women experience these feelings as quite unpleasant;
- Not usually available for use during second stage;
- The face mask can be awkward or unpleasant.

Epidurals

The epidural has made most other methods of pain relief obsolete in the labour process. However, there are considerations that some women don't take into account when choosing to have an epidural.

A common description of the procedure: *(variations of the procedure do occur)*

Before you receive an epidural, you will get a litre of intravenous fluids to build up your blood volume and prevent the decrease in blood pressure that sometimes accompanies an epidural. Your doctor or anesthesiologist will then ask you to sit or lie on your side and curl into the knee-chest position to round your lower back. This widens the space between the vertebrae, making it easier to find the right area for injection. As your doctor or midwife rubs your lower back with an antiseptic solution, it will feel cold. Next, you will feel a slight stinging sensation as the doctor injects some local anesthetic under your skin to numb the area. When the area is sufficiently numb, he or she will insert a larger needle into the epidural space in the spine and inject a test dose to determine if the needle is in the right place and ensure that you are not allergic to the medication. Once the needle is properly inserted, the doctor threads a plastic catheter through the needle into the epidural space and removes the needle, leaving the flexible catheter in place. The pain reliever you and your doctor have decided on is then fed into the catheter. A few minutes later you may feel a shooting sensation, like an electric shock, down one leg. Within five minutes you are likely to begin to feel numb from your navel down, or you may notice that your legs are feeling warm and/or tingly. Within 10-20 minutes the lower half of your body will feel partially or completely numb, depending on the type of epidural used, and the pain of surges will subside.

The exact level of loss of sensation cannot be predicted precisely. Most mothers experience numbness from the navel down, some experience loss of sensation as high as the nipples. A few mothers notice some patchy areas on their skin where they can still feel sensations. There are also times when epidurals don't work, or only work on one side of the body – talk with your doctor about the possible problems and risks associated with epidurals.

This is the point where women either want to hug their anesthetist or wish they had a different choice because they find themselves as a passive patient rather than in control of an active birth

Advantages of epidurals

- Epidurals nearly always give good pain relief;
- Because the drugs used are injected into your back, very little goes through to your baby; and
- An epidural can help to control your blood pressure if it is a little high while you are in labour.

Disadvantages of epidurals

- Your blood pressure might drop, which can make you feel sick and dizzy.
- Your labour may slow down and you might be offered Syntocinon to speed things up again.
- Your mobility is likely to be limited, however, this will vary as to the type of epidural used. Discuss your options with your anesthetist and ask what to expect.
- You may not be able to pass urine. If this happens a small tube (catheter) will be used to empty your bladder.
- There is an increased chance of your doctor needing to use forceps or the vacuum to assist you in birthing your baby.

Unlikely but possible side effects:

- A small number of women develop a severe headache following an epidural, usually this can be treated effectively fairly quickly, but it can sometimes last for a number of weeks.
- For a small number of women the epidural only relieves pain on one side of the body or doesn't work at all. There are also occasionally problems with insertion of the needle into the epidural space.
- Epidural sometimes leads to a high temperature, which could lead to an abnormally fast heart rate in your baby. This may lead to you and/or your baby being treated with antibiotics and screened for infection.
- Some women get an itchy feeling from the drugs used, if this happens ask if the combination of drugs can be altered to help relieve this.

Some of the disadvantages of having an epidural are less likely to be a problem if the epidural is not commenced in early labour. And with all of the preparation that you and your partner are currently undertaking and the choices you have already made, it is unlikely that you will be choosing an epidural in the midst of a normal labour.

There is an art, I'm sure, in providing you with just enough aesthetic for pain relief, but not so much that it interferes with your labour.

Narcotic Pain Relief (e.g. Pethidine)

Narcotic analgesics (such as pethidine) relieve pain by blocking the pain receptors in the brain. Analgesics affect people differently. Not only does the degree of pain relief narcotics provide vary from woman to woman, so do the mental and emotional side effects. Some mothers feel total relief within 20 minutes of the dose, some report only slight relief. Others report little relief at all, claiming the foggy mind was worse than a hurting body. Some women enjoy the euphoria narcotics can cause; a floaty feeling that helps them take their mind off their labour. Other mothers find narcotics compromise their ability to make decisions that benefit the progress of their labour. If a mother's mind is too muddled to participate in managing her labour with movement and changes of position, her labour may be prolonged, as will her pain. Narcotics can also make you feel very sleepy, so much so that you sleep between surges and wake only as each one peaks, unable to focus and work with your breath.

The best time to administer narcotics is when your labour is very active (6-8 centimetres), just before you enter transition, or if your surges become so overwhelming that you are losing control. Because the effect of pethidine on a newborn's nervous and respiratory systems peaks around two hours after they are given, doctors prefer not to give these drugs within two hours of when they expect you to birth. They want to give the drug time to wear off, at least to the point that it does not compromise baby's ability to breathe after birth. Thus, doctors will generally not feel it is safe to give pethidine once the pushing stage has begun. Fortunately, once you have the urge to push, your need for medical pain relief will be greatly diminished. Don't worry too much, however, if a situation arises in which you must have a narcotic pain reliever during the pushing stage; baby can be given an injection of a narcotic blocker (Narcan) immediately after birth, which reverses the effect of the drug on baby's ability to breathe.

Two concerns:
- When analgesic drugs act on the pain pathways in the woman's brain, they also cross over the placenta to your baby's brain affecting heart beat and respiration rates.

- These drugs also affect the mind, impairing the ability to focus. This may affect how you are able to manage the surges, especially if the drug has not taken away all of the pain. You might also find that bonding and breastfeeding are affected if you and your baby are both still groggy after birth.

ACTIVE MANAGEMENT OF THIRD STAGE

Active management of the third stage of labour involves an injection of Syntocinon given to the mother as or just after the baby is born to speed up the separation of the placenta and hasten its arrival. The injection is also given to reduce the chance of hemorrhage after the birth. The injection is used in the third stage of labour to ensure that the uterus continues to surge effectively in order to easily expel the placenta .Breastfeeding is the natural alternative as the stimulation of the nipple encourages the mother's body to continue the release of oxytocin and thus encourages the uterus to release the placenta and return to its pre-pregnancy size).

When is it necessary?

- History of obstetric difficulties (for example previous post-partum hemorrhage, incoordinate uterine contractions).
- Low hemoglobin levels in the blood (anemia) , which could mean delay in blood clotting.
- Following a Caesarean section.

How is it done?

- The Syntocinon can be given either by injection, usually into the mother's thigh after the baby is born, or if a drip line is in place, through the drip directly into a vein. The injection by needle is very quick and with a fine needle, some women don't even realise they have had the injection as they are too busy bonding with their new baby.
- The cord should be clamped before the injection is given so there is no need to worry about any of the hormone crossing to your baby.
- The cord is gently tugged to encourage early separation and delivery of the placenta.

Benefits:

- The third stage of labour can be completed quite quickly and with little chance of complication.

- There will be less bleeding immediately after the birth (i.e. reduced risk of hemorrhaging)..
- There will be much less chance of needing an internal, manual cleaning of the uterus (commonly referred to as a 'd & c') to remove any remaining placenta (which could lead to serious infection).

Some things to consider:

- The delivery of the placenta must be completed before the uterus contracts far enough to trap the placenta behind the closing cervix. Once the injection is given, the placenta must be delivered within 10 minutes to prevent this happening. It might be good to ask if you can have at least 20 minutes after your baby is born to give your body a chance to deliver the placenta naturally. However, it is also important to know that the majority of women who do hemorrhage, do so within the first few minutes after birth. Talk to your doctor so that you can make and informed choice.
- Excessive pulling on the cord in an attempt to deliver the placenta can, in rare cases, cause the cord to break, remind your doctor or midwife to tug *gently*.
- If the placenta did become trapped in the uterus, a manual removal under general anesthetic would be needed. The doctor uses her hand to scrape the placenta off the uterine wall and bring it out through the vagina. This could happen with or without the Syntocinon being administered. Talk to your doctor about the risks.
- If there is an undiagnosed twin present, giving Syntocinon may cause the second twin to be caught inside the uterus. A Caesarean section or general anesthetic may be needed to deliver the second baby, a very rare event.
- High levels of artificial oxytocin may cause reduced sensitivity to natural levels of oxytocin released in response to sucking on the breast by the baby. In some instances, this could lead to difficulties with the let-down reflex and establishment of lactation in the first few days post-partum. This has not been sufficiently researched to know whether it is a common problem or not.

UNDERSTANDING BREECH BABIES

In the past medical professional have quoted studies that showed that breech babies have a lower risk of birth injury and newborn complications if delivered surgically rather than vaginally. The main concern in the vaginal delivery of a breech newborn is that, with the feet or buttocks presenting first, the head will not have enough time to mould itself to the pelvic canal and may get stuck once the rest of the body is out. Also, a breech delivery can cause damage to the major nerves leading to the arms and hands. Both of these complications are less likely when baby presents buttocks first rather than feet first (frank breech).

However, with baby in the breech position it does not mean you must have a caesarean birth. There are midwives who still posses the skills required to birth a baby in the breech position, comfortably and naturally. The main thing is to find a midwife who is both experienced and confident in natural breech births and who understands the difference between a breech 'delivery' and a breech 'birth'. Many women who have birthed a baby in the breech position vaginally have said that it is basically pain-free and far more comfortable to have a soft little bottom wriggle its way out first than a hard head!

There are also a few obstetricians who will attend vaginal births for breech babies in selective situations, deemed by them to be safe. Your doctor will weigh the risks of the surgical versus the vaginal birth and recommend the course of action that is best in your situation. Remember that most obstetricians are weighing up legal considerations as well as your birthing choices.

There are alternatives to explore with your midwife or doctor that may make it possible to deliver your baby naturally:

- Focus on the very real possibility that your baby might turn. Around half of all babies start out bottom down early in pregnancy. Most turn head-down by 32-34 weeks. For some unknown reason, three to four percent of babies never turn head- down. One study found that 82% of breech babies turned after hypnosis for the presentation while only 47% of the babies in the non-hypnosis group turned (Mehl, 1994).

- Try self-hypnosis or work with a professional;
- Acupuncture is very effective for some women;
- Swimming, hand-stands and somersaults in the pool can encourage some babies to turn;
- Slant-lying, find a way to lay with your head lower than your abdomen and feet. Spend 10-15 minutes in this position each day until you feel your baby turn. Be very careful getting up from this position, you may need to take just as long to get up to allow the blood to flow back down from your head to avoid a thumping head ache.
- Crawling on the floor using the Alexander Technique;
- Osteopathy can work if you think tight back muscles might be holding baby upright.
- If your baby hasn't turned on her own by 36-37 weeks, your doctor (or a specialist you are referred to) can attempt a maneuver called external version (ECV), in which he or she manipulates your abdomen to turn baby into the head-down position. External version is successful 60 to 70 percent of the time (40-50 percent for first pregnancies), but some babies turn back and require a second attempt.
- Search out a midwife or doctor who has experience in vaginal birth of babies in breech position and discuss the possibilities.

Note from Shari: my second bub was still breech at almost 39 weeks, I had tried swimming, acupuncture, slant-lying, crawling for weeks. On the advice of my midwife I was booked in for an ECV, I went home that afternoon and focused on my bub, asking her to turn, visualising and connecting with her. Later that evening my husband took me through my breech turn hypnosis script that I had used successfully with many other women. When we arrived at the hospital for the ECV I didn't mention to anyone that I thought our baby was now head down, but I wasn't at all surprised when the obstetrician announced that the ECV wouldn't be necessary! I felt an amazing sense of accomplishment and connection with my bub and had a strong sense that hers would be a good birth.

UNDERSTANDING CAESAREAN BIRTHS

If you are reading this book you are most likely someone who believes that caesarean birth is primarily an emergency procedure to be used in situations where it is not possible to achieve the end goal of **healthy mum, healthy baby** by pursuing a vaginal birth.

You are also probably aware of the gulf of misunderstanding that exists between women who choose an elective caesarean and women who choose natural birth. The two groups of women have different priorities, philosophies and perspectives and there is little use in one trying to convince the other of right and wrong.

If you are planning and preparing for a natural, drug-free vaginal birth it is still wise to be aware of some of the factors that can lead to and are involved in caesarean birth , just in case labour goes a little pear-shaped and an unpredictable circumstance arises. It is good to have thought through plan 'b' (or 'z' as the case may be), so that you can still make it a positive and welcoming experience, for you and your baby.

The most common reasons for emergency caesarean births are:

- **Slow to progress** (or failure to progress) - which accounts for a large proportion of caesarean deliveries. It means that labour doesn't progress according to the usual or textbook timetable. For various reasons the cervix does not open enough and/or the baby does not descend. Some cases of slow to progress cannot be avoided, such as a very short umbilical cord, however, many instances could have been avoided if the woman and her partner had been made aware of the effects of the fight or flight response on labour.

- Avoiding a caesarean as a result of "slow to progress" is very much in your control. You are now aware of and understand how to avoid the fight or flight response and with good emotional and physical support there will be very little impeding your progress. All of your relaxation and natural methods for managing the labour process will prevent stalling or pausing of the labour process. However, if you find that your body takes a break from the hard work of the surges, you and your partner also have the confidence to ask for more time if there is any pressure to speed things up. If appropriate, as a back-up tactic, ask for Syntocinon or other methods of inducing labour to be tried and exhausted before a caesarean is performed – remembering your goal at all times *health mum, healthy baby.*

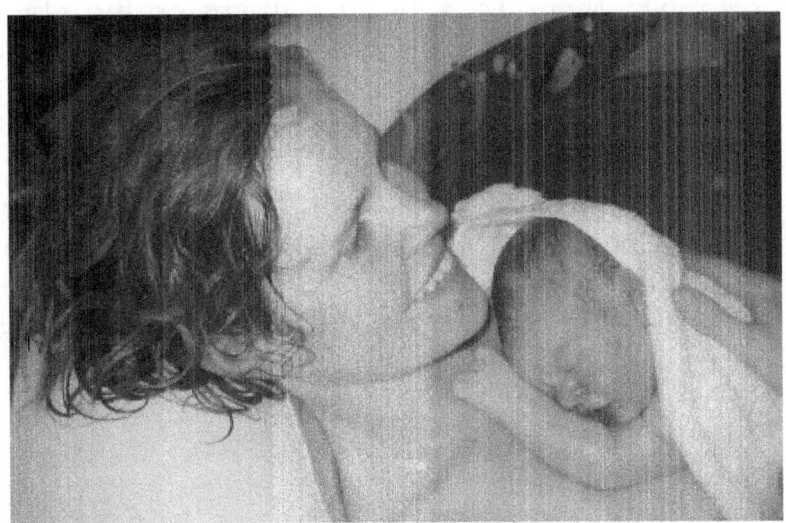

- **Repeat caesarean** - is the most common reason for this type of birth. Vaginal birth after caesarean (VBAC) is now considered safe in the right circumstances, speak with your midwife or doctor to find out if you might be able to try for a vaginal birth despite a previous caesarean. A calm, relaxed and well informed mum, supported by a like-minded partner, are very strong candidates for a VBAC (read Erika's story at the beginning of the book).

- **Fetal distress** - is the third most common situation leading to a caesarean delivery. Fetal heart patterns on the electronic fetal monitor may suggest that baby's well-being is in jeopardy unless he or she is delivered quickly. A fetal heart rate that is higher or lower than average is a sign that baby may not be getting enough oxygen or is not recovering well from the decreased heart rate that is normal during contractions. While some of the reasons babies receive insufficient oxygen are beyond your influence, choices you make in labour help determine your baby's well-being. Remember that in normal circumstances your breathing and relaxation can help prevent this situation from arising.

- **Cephalopelvic disproportion (CPD)** - is another reason for caesarean births. This means that the baby is too big to pass through the pelvic outlet, a relatively rare occurrence. Labouring and delivering in a more upright position, especially squatting, can enlarge the pelvic outlet, often allowing even a small woman to deliver a big baby. With the right care and support during labour, most women are physically able to birth their babies vaginally.

Whatever choices you make and whatever turn your birthing takes remember your goal, a healthy baby in your arms – this is the only thing that you need to focus on.

If you focus on welcoming your baby rather than birthing your baby then there can be no failure or disappointment.

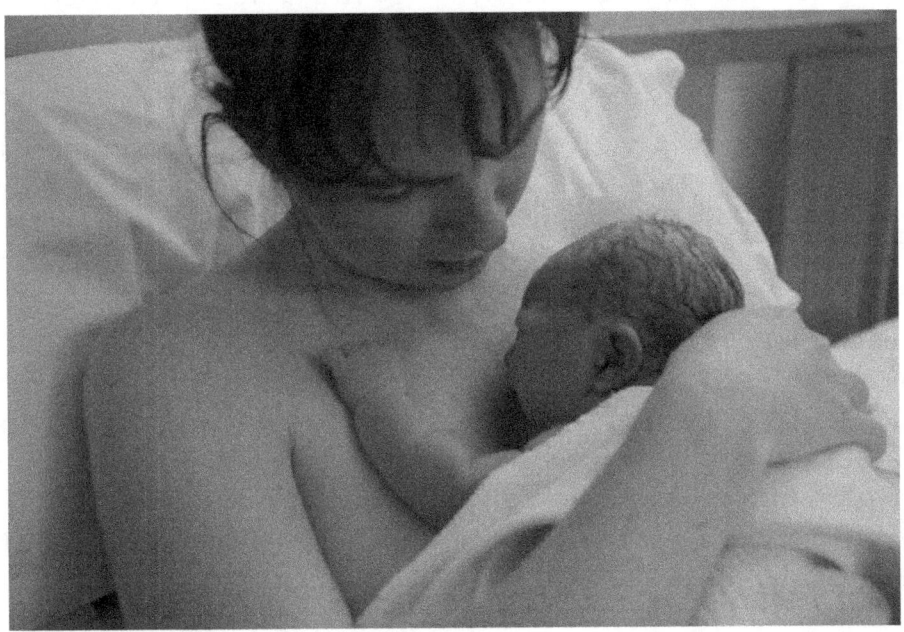

Ways To Make Caesarean Delivery Memorable:

- Ask your doctor for a spinal or epidural anesthetic so you can be awake for the birth (this is generally routine procedure, unless there is a medical reason why an epidural cannot be given ,a general anesthetic will not be used).

- Use your relaxation techniques to stay calm during your preparations. Play your music and take in your essential oils on a tissue under your pillow.

- Have your partner sit next to you at the head of the operating table. If he's hesitant, remind him that the actual procedure takes place behind a sterile curtain. He won't see anything upsetting.

- Ask your obstetrician to lift baby high enough so you can see him or her right after delivery. It is a beautiful sight to see your newborn lifted "up and out" during a caesarean birth.

- Ask that your baby be given to you as soon as possible. Sometime baby might need to be quickly checked over (temperature, breathing and pulse, and heart rates are stable) but ask that baby be brought to you asap to be held and hugged for that very important skin-to-skin contact. You may need some help since you may be a bit groggy and one arm may be immobilized for an IV. Treat this mother- father-baby bonding time just as you would have after a vaginal birth (and don't forget the photos).

- While your uterus and abdomen are being stitched closed (this takes about 30 minutes) and the operation completed, your partner should accompany baby to the nursery so he or she will not be alone with strangers. This extra father- baby bonding time will have a deep impact on both of them. Use your self-hypnosis and relaxation techniques to remain calm and confident while this is happening.

- To decrease postoperative pain, ask your anesthesiologist about using a do-it-yourself analgesia, called "patient-controlled analgesia" (PCA). This is set up so you can administer your own medication through your intravenous line. Just turn the pump on and off, as you need relief. This medication is safe for your breastfeeding baby. Additionally, use your self-hypnosis techniques to help you relax so that your body can focus on healing.

- In most cases baby can be brought to your bedside almost immediately after the surgery is complete. The best postoperative "pain reliever" is an "injection" of baby in your arms.

#4 Checking in – Self-Awareness Exercise.

Thinking about labour and birthing, on a scale from 0 to 100, where 0 represents not at all and 100 means completely, how would you rate yourself <u>right now</u> in terms of:

0   100
_____

CONFIDENCE

0   100
_____

CALMNESS

Place a mark on the lines above to indicate how you feel <u>right now</u>

Thinking about labour and birthing, on a scale from 0 to 100, where 0 represents not at all and 100 means completely, how would you <u>want to feel during labour and birthing</u> in terms of:

0   100
_____

CONFIDENCE

0   100
_____

CALMNESS

Place a mark on the lines above to indicate how you <u>want to feel right now</u>

Has there been any change since you last rated yourself?

Is there any difference between the two sets of ratings this time?

If yes, why do you think that the ratings are different?

It might be useful to make some notes about how you are feeling now and what needs to change (if anything) in order for you to be feeling the way you want to be feeling. Notice your thoughts and feelings, beliefs and knowledge and how prepared you feel.

What are you in control of? What things are you able to change in order to feel calmer and/or more confident about birthing?

CHAPTER 5 WELCOME

Armed with Awareness, feeling Trust in your body that it can do the Work that needs to be done, and having made the Choices that you feel are right for your and your baby, all there is left to do is Welcome this new little person into the world.

Begin to think about how you would like to welcome your baby into the world. If you were this little baby, how would you like things to be when you first looked around, what would you like to see, feel, smell, hear and taste?

Birth Plans and Preferences

Use your birth plan and preferences, not only to prepare yourself and your partner for a positive experience but also to plan for how you are going to celebrate and welcome this little person on their Birth-Day.

Following are a few suggestions for birth plans and preferences.

Many women, after all of their reading and research, preparing and pondering find themselves with a head full of information about labour and birthing. When they write out their birth plan, end up with a 5-6 page script.

Good.

Use this as an exercise to get all of your information and ideas out on paper. Then you can sort through it, identify any gaps in your knowledge and be well-prepared for your ideal birthing experience. Another excellent reason for allowing yourself the luxury of a 5 page birth plan is that your partner will then have the opportunity to take the script and get a good understanding of just what you are hoping for and how he might play an active role in helping you to get what you want.

Once your partner has had a chance to read through your plan, sit down with it together and find out if he has any input or special requests. Although most men will thrown their hands in the air and exclaim that it's you that has to do all of the hard work so they'll just 'fit in' with whatever you want. It is a good reminder for both of you that this is his baby too and he might have a preference for the type of music playing just as or just after your baby is born. And unless you ask ,can you be really sure whether or not he wants to cut the cord (or even receive the baby)?

Once you have chatted about the plan and negotiated your way through your combined CD collection...then it is time to prepare your birthing preferences.

Take the birthing plan and go through it together to find the 5 or 6 things in the plan that are most important to you. You might start out with a list of 12 or even 20 items, cut it down as much as you can to the things that matter most about the way you want your baby to be welcomed. If you can't get it down to one concise, outline style page – no problem, depending on who you have chosen to work with some obstetricians and most midwives will find a more personal and detailed briefing about your preferences helpful.

The advantages to the one pager list of preferences is that your health care providers will get a feel for your wishes easily (can be an important point at 3am),. It might just make it that much more likely to entice someone to cooperate with special requests.

Don't shy away from writing a birth plan or birthing preferences because you are worried about feeling like you are telling the obstetrician or midwife how to do their jobs. As a result of your conversations throughout pregnancy your doctor or midwife should already be familiar with your views and approach to birthing. However, some of the details may have never been discussed and the written birth plan or list of preferences can help to finalize these. Doctors and midwives are professionals who want to do their job well. You can help them to do this by providing them with information about what you are wanting from them. How they can help you to have the best experience possible – in your eyes. They want you to walk away happy and telling people about what a great job they did, but they can't know how best to do this for you unless you tell them. Prepare your birthing preferences for this reason.

Remember, there is no need to include preferences that are sure to be irrelevant. For example, most hospitals no longer do routine enemas and pubic shaves; therefore, there is no need to write a request that it not be done.

Use your Birthing Plan to:

- get things clear in your mind;
- identify any gaps in knowledge about processes, procedures or policies;
- walk yourself through your ideal birth;
- ensure your partner is clear about your expectations of them;
- ensure you have decided which techniques you will use and when;
- ensure your partner is aware of the choices you are making;
- prepare for 'plan b' should the need arise; and
- plan for all of the details and specifics of your baby's Birth Day.

Prepare your Birthing Preferences to:

- communicate to your doctor or midwife about the factors that are most important to you about your birthing;
- ensure that your doctor or midwife understand how you would like to welcome your baby;
- let your doctor or midwife know about any special requests.

Remember – the best laid plans can still come undone. Some doctors and midwives don't like birth plans because they worry that the woman believes that this is how it MUST be and any deviation from the plan is a failure or violation. This is why it can be good to also consider your *preferences* in different circumstances and include 'plan b' in your birth plan. Still *plan* for your ideal birth - with good preparation it is likely that your plan will be realised.

A Sample of the Birthing Preferences that you might like to give to your Dr or midwife is presented:

Dear Dr/Midwife

*My Partner and I have chosen to birth our baby with the calm and relaxed techniques learnt in our **BirthSkills** program. From everything that we have learnt, we are aware that we have choices during our birthing, we are aware that medical intervention might be necessary if our birthing takes an unexpected turn. We are prepared for whatever turn our birthing takes and know that you will have our full cooperation once we fully understand the nature of the circumstance.*

We believe and trust that you will do everything in your power to help us to welcome our baby in the most calm, comfortable and naturally satisfying way possible. We believe in natural birth and trust the ability of the mother's body to do this.

These are our birthing preferences, thank you for honouring our requests:

- *Please do not offer medication for pain relief, I will ask for it if I feel it is necessary. I will be using hypnosis techniques, physical relaxation and hydrotherapy to keep me comfortable.*
- *Please help us by leaving our music playing and oils burning at all times.*
- *We would like a quiet and private atmosphere in which to birth our baby.*
- *Please offer suggestions for positioning during the birthing of my baby to make it easier for my baby to make its way into the world.*
- *Please explain fully, any procedure or intervention that might become necessary and the reason for this. We will make the best decision for our baby and ourselves.*
- *Please place my baby up on my (or mother's name) bare chest immediately after it is born.*

Thank you, for helping us to create a calm, gentle and welcoming birthing day for our new baby.

Warm Regards,

New Mum & Dad

PREPARING YOUR LABOUR NEST

As well as addressing all of the choices you have for labour, medical and natural, use your planning to identify the things that you might like to take in with you for labour and birth.

It might be nice to think of the labour suite at the hospital as a 'nest', or simply think about the physical environment that you would like to create. Think about choosing items that are going to help you have the experience you are hoping for.

It might also be good to choose at least one item for each of your senses so that your entire existence in that space is in harmony with your image of your ideal birth.

For example – of your image of an ideal birth is calm, quiet and relaxed you might choose the following conditions or items to take in with you:

- **Sight**: take in a picture of your favourite place in nature, holiday destination or simply use a visualization of this place, make posters of your favourite affirmations;
- **Sound**: take in music that is calming and soothing. It might be music that you and your partner have enjoyed together in the past or special music that you have chosen for your baby;
- **Smell**: you might like to take in essential oils or even a flower that you associate with feeling relaxed, clothes or blankets from home are also important to provide a familiar smell for your baby.
- **Taste**: BYO snacks (fuel)! If you are having cravings for a particular food or drink, take it in with you to ensure a reliable supply! As well as satisfying cravings, it is important that you 're-fuel' during labour with nutritious food that will keep up your energy levels.
- **Touch**: many women enjoy taking in their own pillow or wearing their own comfy clothes during labour. And don't forget the wonderful touch of massage!

Experiment with your tools. Be sure to experiment with your bag of tricks at home to see what you think will work. Once you're in labour, let your instincts guide you in choosing what will be helpful at the time. Many women using the relaxation techniques outlined in this book find that labour progresses so well they don't get time to use half of the things they prepared!

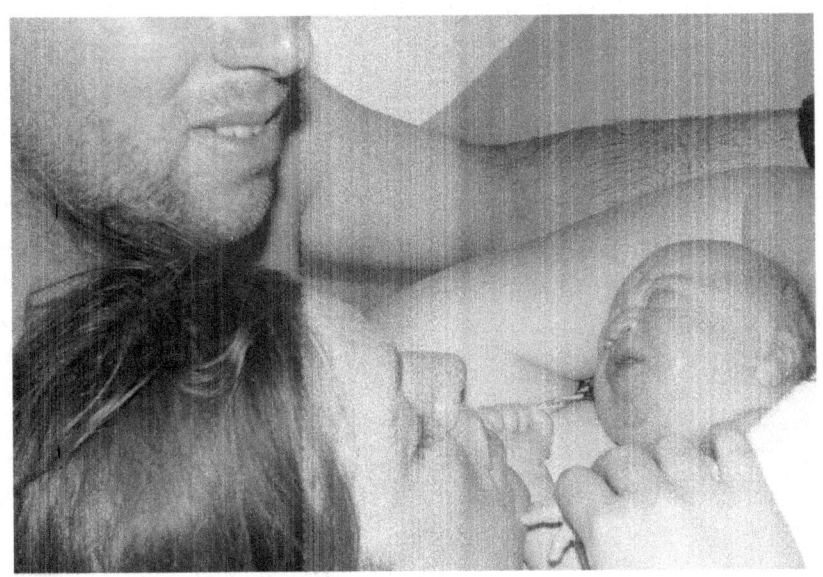

Some other suggestions for creating your own special birthing environment:

- **Bring music to birth by.** Studies show that mothers using music during labour required fewer pain-relieving drugs than mothers who did not listen to music. As music stimulates a mother's body to release endorphins, the natural pain-relieving and relaxing hormones. Most birthing suites will have a CD player but it's worth checking before the day.

- **Essential oils.** Aromatherapy is another means of filling your senses with pleasant stimuli. Essential oils can be used during labour for relaxation, to stimulate the uterine surges or to refresh and uplift the atmosphere. Use the oils carefully, making sure you have done some research before labour, knowing which oils are safe to use and which to avoid. The easiest way of using the oils is in an electric vaporiser (candles are not allowed in the birthing suites due to the presence of the gas). If your membranes haven't released add a few drops of oil to the bath (but not if you plan to birth in the bath), or use an essential oil infused shower gel, massage oil or add a few drops to a hot or cold compress.

- **Birth ball.** Usually 64cm physiotherapy or fit-ball, which naturally relaxes the pelvic muscles and opens the bony pelvis when you sit on it. Sitting on the ball also has the added benefit of massaging the perineum as you roll around.

- **Your own pillows and doona.** Hospitals have plenty of pillows on hand (your partner might have to put in a special request for extra - don't be shy in asking) but you might like to take a favourite with you. The smell of home or the sight of your favourite pillowcase can bring a sense of comfort that might help you to get a few moments sleep between surges.

- **Try a hot and/or cold compress.** Hot packs improve blood flow to tissues; cold packs lessen pain perception in these tissues. You will need both kinds. A hot water bottle or a rubber surgical glove filled with warm water is a fine hot-pack. Nestle against your lower abdomen, groin, or thigh to relieve achy muscles or just to relax you. Try a warm face cloth on your perineum to help prepare the area for stretching. Packs of frozen veggies, covered with a cloth, work well as cold packs to soothe a hot forehead or numb an aching back (and good for the perineum after birth).

- **BYO**. If you have been having a hankering for a particular type of juice or fruit; pack an Eski and take it to the hospital with you. I drank two litres of blackcurrant juice and ate two sandwiches and a muesli bar, during my first stage of labour (8 hours). When you are relaxed and calm during labour your body will still be able to digest and will benefit greatly from the fluids and energy, from sipping and nibbling.

The principle underlying the preparation of a birthing plan or preference is that you have thought about the labour process and how you would like to welcome your baby. On the day just go with whatever is working for you, let go of any plans and do what feels good or right. A visualisation that you have never practiced or thought about might come to you, the bath or massage might be totally annoying or you might find yourself birthing in a position you had never thought of....prepare yourself and your tools, then ... let go and be open to the experience.

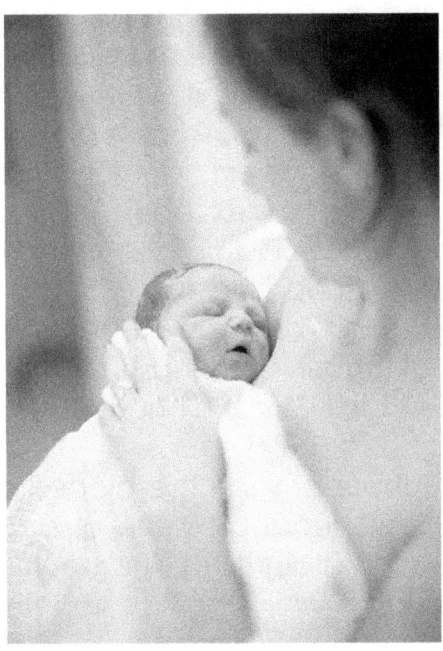

WELCOME – THE FOUR STAGES OF LABOUR

Every labour is different. Situations vary from woman to woman and from labour to labour. Use the **BirthSkills CD** to help you to prepare, mentally and emotionally, for this amazing journey.

You will mostly hear people talking about the first two stages of labour - first stage begins with the opening of the cervix; and the second stage involves the baby moving down through the birth canal (the vagina) and culminates in birth. The third stage is when the placenta and uterus lining are expelled and the fourth stage is bonding and possibly some postpartum procedures.

In Summary:

- **The first stage of labour** is generally the longest, taking an average of 8-16 hours for a first baby and 3-10 hours for a second or subsequent baby (these are very general figures). As a pregnancy nears its end, the cervix becomes softer, thinner and shorter in a process known as "ripening". This is followed by the opening of the cervix known as "dilation" and is estimated in centimetres. Once dilation reaches around 4cm, labour is said to be established," and said to be "progressing" as it continues to open. Full dilation is estimated to be about 10cm. **Transition** occurs towards the end of the first stage when the cervix is open at about 8cm. It is the part of labour that is often the most uncomfortable as the muscles of the uterus are doing the final bit of stretching to pull the cervix open and at the same time, starting the process of nudging baby down and out; at this stage muscles are often fatigued and trying to do two jobs at once, easy to see why this might be uncomfortable for a bit.
- **The second stage of labour** is the 'pushing' bit and ends with your baby coming out – usually around 1hour but could be as quick as a few minutes or as long as 2-3 hours.
- **The third stage of labour** is when the placenta comes out and is often not even acknowledged by the overwhelmed parents as they emotionally skip straight to the **fourth stage of labour**, bonding with their baby.

The First Stage of Labour

If you are expecting your first baby, you may notice pressure in your groin and on your bladder beginning up to four weeks before the birth. Your baby's head might become engaged in your pelvis in preparation for labour. The first stage of labour often begins with the loss of the mucus plug from the entrance of the cervix. This might be bloodstained or pinkish in colour, or clear like the discharge at ovulation, and is called a 'show', and may occur several days before labour begins. This is completely normal.

The amniotic membrane may leak or break and the waters either trickle or gush out, commonly known as the waters breaking (or this may not happen until the moment you baby is about to be born). The amount of fluid coming out at this stage will depend on how fully engaged your baby's head is. The amniotic fluid replenishes every three hours so there is no danger of your baby being 'high and dry'. Once your surges have begun, they will probably become more regular and closer together.

During this stage, surges might occur 5-20 minutes apart and last for 30 – 60 seconds. Some women experience 'pre labour' where surges start then stop for a period before beginning again (this could go on for days).

As the surges strengthen and the interval between them decreases, you may find yourself retreating into a meditative state. Your breathing pattern may become your focus and your primary means of managing any discomfort.

At this stage the muscles at the top of your uterus are pressing down on your baby's bottom and his head is pressing against your cervix. As the baby's head descends, it exerts pressure on the cervix, assisting further dilation. Dilation of the cervix may not occur at a constant rate. Usually, the dilation from 1-5cm takes much longer than from 5-10cm. Generally, the stronger and longer the surges, the more responsive the cervix will be in dilating. Surges are generally at their strongest near the end of the first stage of labour (during transition) as the cervix opens wider. Once dilation reaches 10cm, the first stage is complete.

Near Complete (Transition)

Transition is the point when the labour reaches a peak before shifting gears. This part can last for an hour or two or be over in a flash, though is usually longer during the first labour. This is the part of labour that women often remember as the most difficult, despite it often being just 20 minutes or so, this is the time when feelings of defeat or misery may set in; "I don't think I can do this for much longer", "I've had enough , someone get this baby out of me". But with a well prepared partner, this is the time to re-focus and prepare to meet your baby. Being reminded of your favourite affirmation, getting into the shower and thinking about what is actually happening in your body will all help to keep you focused during this challenge.

As transition changes into second stage there may be feelings of rectal pressure (feeling like you need to or are doing a poo) as your baby's head descends into the vaginal canal and takes up room, squashing the wall of the rectum. Use this time to re-establish your relaxation and breathing patterns, to prepare the oil burner or music that you want when your baby is born. Use the bath, shower or massage to help you stay calm and prepare to welcome your baby.

Birthing (The Second Stage of Labour)

Now begins the second stage when you will begin to bear down. Surges might occur 2-5 minutes apart and last for as long as 60-90 seconds. You will probably have an overwhelming urge to bear down and push the baby through the birth canal (though don't worry if this doesn't happen, everything is still working fine). During the descent, the rotation of your baby's head is assisted by powerful surges, stretching the vagina open to accommodate its passage. The bones of your baby's skull are soft enough to allow some flexibility and the limbs will be tucked tightly in. The natural action of a surging uterus will mould the baby into the right shape for its journey through the vaginal canal.

This stage of labour can arouse feelings of passion and excitement and you might experience an increase of energy. You will most likely experience a natural response to the energy sweeping through your body. Use your breath and trust the spontaneous feelings. Some people think it is a good idea to hold your breath then push aggressively, however it's been found that holding your breath is not only exhausting for the mother, but can be dangerous for the baby in that it reduces the oxygen content of the blood.

Keep visualizing the breath going down to your baby and gently helping to nudge your baby down. Once your cervix is fully dilated it is only a very short journey to the outside world (around 10cm). Visualize the birth path opening up, the baby coming down easily and working with your body, listening to your body, breathing your baby down. You might feel the need to bear down and push. You can work with your surges to push if you need to but you must keep breathing and not push aggressively unless your Dr or midwife instructs you to do so. Relax, allow your body to do its job. Trust that you body is birthing your baby. Breathe with your body, offering the resources you have, use your inner wisdom to know what your body needs from your mind.

Take a quick, strong breath in because you are working harder now and want to sustain a good movement down. Focus your breath, and your mind, down into your vagina. You may experience the feeling of wanting to move your bowels. Your baby is pushing on the outside wall of the bowels, giving you that sensation, this is good, your baby is moving down and out.

The pelvic floor muscles are designed in a sling-shape. As your baby comes down it flattens the bowel as it moves around and under the pubic arch. There might be a lot of pressure in your bottom. Know that your baby is very close. When you take a breath in, it's slightly different now, previously you were breathing deeply through the waves now it is time to work with them. So take a good breath in and nudge that baby down. Eyes gently closed if you want to or open, but visualizing your baby moving down. You will try to get 3 or 4 sustained nudges with each surge. Don't be tempted to take a short shallow breath, your body and your baby need oxygen. Sustain your nudging for the duration of your surge and gradually the uterus will gently guide your baby down.

The uterus is still playing a major role, you are helping to maximise each surge with your breath, remembering to keep your bottom and your legs as relaxed as possible. Imagine your breath nudging your baby down. It is so important to listen to your body, if it is telling you to nudge then nudge, don't try to move your baby down when your body is not in surge. Your vagina is going to open, to stretch as you slowly nudge your baby down, using the breathing, using visualisations.

Keeping your body loose is very important and this way you will avoid any unnecessary tearing or cutting. Your breathing and visualization are so important at this stage. Be excited and put all fear aside as you prepare to welcome your baby.

As your baby's head passes through the bony pelvic outlet, her head must twist sideways slightly then to a backwards-facing position again before becoming visible. Seen for the first time, it may look more like a wrinkled walnut than a baby's head. When the widest part of the baby's head is at the birth opening, you will feel stretched to your utmost. This is known as the "crowning". It is important not to push too hard at this stage, despite wanting to, as you may tear the perineal tissue. Let your midwife guide you through this process.

The doctor or midwife may consider it necessary to perform an episiotomy at this stage. If you do not wish to have one, say so. To avoid tearing, you will need to begin long, slow breathing before the head crowns in a bid to "breathe the baby out" rather than pushing. The doctor or midwife will check to see that the umbilical cord is free of your baby's neck and may use a catheter in your baby's mouth to suck out any mucus.

Your baby's head may look sticky with mucus and violet or purple in colour though this is normal as your baby has yet to take its first breath. Once her head is free, it will turn to align with the shoulders, which are still inside. You may be asked to push to free the shoulders. Next the body will slide out easily and your baby is born. This is often accompanied by a great gush of water, and followed by feelings of great excitement and satisfaction. If you have been calm and quiet throughout labour your baby may not cry at first. Don't be alarmed, sound and movement will come soon.

The baby may be covered in vernix, a creamy-like substance that protects the baby's skin while in the uterus. Its head may be oddly-shaped, asymmetrical and moulded by the birth canal, with a receding forehead and chin. Its face may have little red marks around the eyes and eyelids and its nose may seem flattened. The body, still attached by the umbilical cord, may seem small in comparison with the head, though the genitalia may seem quite large. This is a normal looking baby.

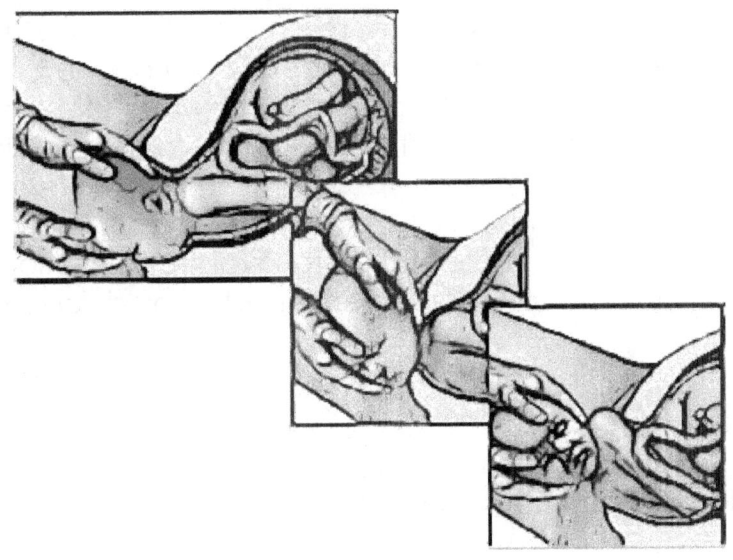

> Your baby's head will turn naturally to the side to allow the shoulders and body to birth. Your Dr or midwife will support your baby's head during the birthing. Once baby's head is safely out Dad might like to take over and receive his baby.

The Third Stage of Labour – Birthing the Placenta

All that remains now within the uterus is the placenta, the attached cord and the remnants of the pregnancy sac. Although you may not feel it, the uterus continues to contract causing the placenta to peel off from the uterine wall. The squeezing of the uterine wall closes off the supply to the blood vessels, preventing excessive bleeding from the wall and keeping blood loss at a minimum. When the placenta is detached, the doctor or midwife may gently pull on the cord and you may be asked to take a breath and bear down a little to assist. Most likely all you will feel is a warm, soft feeling as the placenta slides out.

After it slides out, it will be closely examined by your Dr or midwife to check that every part is there. This is to avoid any section being left within the womb, which if left unnoticed, could cause infection postpartum.

The Fourth Stage - Post Partum Bonding

Most likely you will want to bond with your baby immediately, the vernix can stay on your baby to protect the skin, if you are going to breast feed your baby you may do so as soon as you and the baby are ready. Skin-to-skin contact between mother, baby and father is ideal. Baby can lie up on your chest while your partner gently lays his hand on your baby's back, under the blanket if you are using one. Don't forget to take a moment to connect with your partner at this wonderful time.

Please know, that if you do not feel an instant attachment or bond to your baby, there is nothing wrong with you. This is ok, some women, for a variety of reasons, take longer to feel the deep love and connection between mums and their children. It will come with time, the more you are able to accept that the connection is going to take a bit longer, the faster it will develop. Just care for your baby as best you can, communicate with your partner about your feelings if you can and love will grow naturally when it is the right time for you.

The Placenta

The placenta will look like a big piece of raw liver with a rough side, which was attached to the uterine wall, and a velvety smooth soft side, against which the baby was cushioned. It will have an intricate network of blood vessels, which during pregnancy, was the baby's life support system supplying oxygen and nutrients.

You may want to do something special with your placenta or let it be taken away. If you think you would at least like to see the placenta it might be best to write it down in your birthing preferences so it doesn't disappear without you getting a look at this amazing item.

Cutting the Cord

Once your baby breathes air, it has no further need for the placenta or the umbilical cord. Within a few minutes of the birth, once the cord has stopped pulsating, the cord can be clamped with forceps. Clamps are usually placed at two points, and with a pair of sharp, sterile scissors, the cut is made between these points.

A clamp is then moved closer to the umbilicus (belly button) so the excess cord can be trimmed. There is no hurry for this to be done and there may be some advantages for the baby in waiting for the blood within the cord to drain into its circulation.

Cord Blood Collection

The blood within the umbilical cord is considered to be rich in special blood cells called "stem cells" also found in bone marrow. Stem cells can be used to successfully treat children with leukemia (cancer of the blood cells). For this reason, in some hospitals you may be asked if you would care to donate to a cord blood bank. The collection has to be planned beforehand so that the blood can be collected in a special container and transported to be immediately frozen. The collection process is painless and harmless for both the mother and newborn. In most states of Australia we have the choice of donating the cord blood or storing it for private use if needed.

Repairs to the Perineum

Should your perineum require stitches, suturing is done under local anesthetic and might take a little while, as careful precision is taken in joining together the underlying layers of muscle. An icepack can help reduce swelling. The bloodstained vaginal discharge common following childbirth is called lochia. Some women experience it for just a few days though for others, it may last as long as five or six weeks. It is important to use your bowels as soon as you feel the need to after childbirth, take care to wash the area properly to avoid infection.

The End (actually....The Beginning!)

When you are ready take a shower, this serves the dual purpose of refreshing you and it will give your partner time to bond with his new baby. A long, deep breath and a quiet moment to pat yourself on the back is also deserved. You have just performed one of the most amazing things a person can ever do, and something that no-one else could ever do – given life to <u>your</u> baby!

Congratulations and Enjoy.

#5 Checking in – rating exercise.

Thinking about labour and birthing, on a scale from 0 to 100, where 0 represents not at all and 100 means completely, how would you rate yourself <u>right now</u> in terms of:

0   100
_____

CONFIDENCE

0   100
_____

CALMNESS

Place a mark on the lines above to indicate how you feel <u>right now</u>

Thinking about labour and birthing, on a scale from 0 to 100, where 0 represents not at all and 100 means completely, how would you <u>want to feel during labour and birthing</u> in terms of:

0   100
_____

CONFIDENCE

0   100
_____

CALMNESS

Has there been any change since you last rated yourself?

How do these ratings compare to the first set you did at the beginning of this workbook? If there are still areas you want to work on, go back and ask yourself the questions outlined at the end of module 4.

Recommended Reading:

Birth Without Violence by Frederick Leboyer (2002).

The Waterbirth Book by Janet Balaskas (2004).

Childbirth Without Fear by Dr Grantly Dick-Read (2004).

25 Ways to Awaken Your Birth Power by Danette Watson & Stephanie Corkhill Hyles (2004).

Birth Journeys by Leonie MacDonald (2011).

Alternative Therapies for Pregnancy and Birth by Pat Thomas (2001).

Buddhism for Mothers by Sarah Napthali (2003).

Mindful Motherhood by Cassandra Vieten PhD. (2009).

Appendix – Empowerment Through Natural Therapies

A few suggestions for things to consider and to find out more about:

Nutrition

If you were eating a well-balanced diet before you became pregnant, you probably won't need to make big changes. But some little changes can make a big difference in ensuring that you and your baby get all the vitamins, minerals and calories needed for a healthy pregnancy. Make sure that you are getting food from the five healthy food groups: grain products, vegetables, fruits, protein foods, and milk and milk products. By eating healthy you can contribute to the health and well-being of your child at birth and during breastfeeding.

Following a nutritionally sound diet can better the chances of a normal birth-weight, improved fetal brain development, and decrease the chances of pregnancy complications. Further, eating healthy will benefit you as well as your child. A healthy diet will decrease pregnancy complications in mothers such as anemia, pre-eclampsia, morning sickness, fatigue, and constipation. A healthy diet will also moderate any mood swings and ensure the speediest recovery after your pregnancy. There are many nutrition factors to explore for preventing or managing post-natal depression.

Please avoid caffeine as much as possible, limit to one caffeine drink a day or eliminate completely, and definitely **do not smoke** *during your pregnancy.*

Exercise

With the sedentary lives many of us lead today our bodies are unused to being active. If you are planning an active birth, regular exercise is vital to help you prepare for labour, enhance breathing and circulation, tone and strengthen your muscles and increase flexibility.

Yoga-based exercise is an ideal way to prepare your body and your mind. With practice, positions and movements soon become second nature enabling you to pick and choose the ones that feel most natural and comfortable when you are in labour. Find a good antenatal or pregnancy yoga class if you are interested.

The fit-ball is a wonderful aid to pregnancy exercise. It's particularly useful for strengthening your body's central core - the deep muscles of your abdomen, back and pelvic floor - that is increasingly being recognised by fitness professionals as the foundation of a strong, healthy body.

Weak core muscles can cause your pelvis to tilt forward giving a hollow back posture where your back arches excessively, your belly sags and your bottom sticks out leading to the classic pregnancy "waddling duck" gait.

Strong core muscles help protect your spine, improve balance and posture, aid stability, tone your pelvic floor, lower your risk of back pain and as an added bonus, help your baby adopt the most favourable position for birth.

Other useful pregnancy exercises include walking, pregnancy water aerobics classes, swimming and pilates.

Herbs and Mineral Supplements

Four herbs are particularly recommended by experienced herbalists and have been used safely by pregnant women for centuries. Rich in vitamins and minerals, red raspberry leaf, nettles, alfalfa, and dandelion act as system supporting tonics for overall health of the expectant mother.

- **Red raspberry leaf,** taken as a tea or in capsule form, strengthens the uterus, alleviates morning sickness. It eases labour and delivery as well as postpartum discomforts, and aids in milk productions. Women with a history of miscarriage, however, should not use this herb until the second trimester. Some midwives recommend one cup a day for each trimester i.e. 1 cup a day in 1st trimester, 2 cups a day in 2nd trimester and 3 cups a day in 3rd trimester however, if you are particularly sensitive to the raspberry

leaf and experience surges after drinking the tea do not take it regularly until around week 35 to avoid pre-mature labour.
- **Nettle,** a mineral, is high in calcium, which nourishes both the mother and fetus and can ease painful leg cramps and the pressure of Braxton Hicks. Nettle has been known to improve the elasticity of the veins and strengthen the kidneys. For leg cramps or restless legs **Magnesium** has been found to be particularly beneficial. A magnesium supplements can be taken orally, however, it is best absorbed by the body through the skin. Use magnesium oil or bath salts to soak your feet in or soak your whole body in the bath for 20-30 minutes (remember not to over heat particularly during the first half of your pregnancy).
- **Alfalfa** increases Vitamin K in the blood and used to prevent hemorrhage.
- **Dandelion** strengthens the uterus and kidneys and is high in calcium, potassium, and folic acid.

Great tip from my own wonderful midwife: Use a diluted blend of **Calendula** (marigold extract) and water in a spray bottle to soothe the perineal area after the birth – use as often as you wish!

Please always check with your doctor, midwife or natural health care provider before taking any herbal, mineral or other supplement during pregnancy.

Massage

Pregnancy is a time of major structural, physiological, psychological, spiritual, and social changes. Some of these changes produce discomforts and concerns, which can be addressed with appropriate massage therapy and body use guidance. Pregnancy massage therapy is beneficial throughout the nine months of a low-risk pregnancy. If you are not having a low risk pregnancy, discuss your condition with your obstetrician or midwife. After further discussion, you may be able to receive therapy with additional written release.

Massage therapy in pregnancy can include specific light and deep pressure massage, myofascial techniques, circulatory work, acupressure, reflexology, and other techniques.

Possible Benefits - Massage therapy during pregnancy is not intended to replace appropriate prenatal care. When used as a form of adjunctive health care, some of its possible benefits are:

- Reduces stress and promotes relaxation.
- Provides emotional support and physical nurturing, particularly for those who are alone in the process, either literally or by the emotional absence of the partner.
- Reduces and alleviates neck, back, and joint pain caused by posture, muscle weakness, tension, extra weight, or imbalance.
- Relieves muscle spasms, cramps, and fibrosis.
- Alleviates stress on weight-bearing joints and musculo-fascial structures (sacro-iliac joint, mid-back and lumbar spine, hips).
- Combats tension, fatigue, and headaches, soothe nerves to help with sleep problems, and possibly reduce blood pressure through relaxation and stress reduction.
- Increases blood and lymph circulation and supports the physiological process of gestation, by supporting the work of the heart, increasing cellular respiration, reducing oedema, and contributing to sympathetic nervous system sedation. Reduces the possibility of problems with swelling, varicose veins, and leg cramps.
- Helps maintain skin elasticity to ease stretch marks and uncomfortable tightness.
- Assists with the management of digestive complaints such as constipation, gas, nausea, and indigestion.
- Encourages deeper, easier breathing.
- Enhances self-esteem and self-image, helping the pregnant woman feel more at home in her changing body.
- Develops the sensory awareness and relaxation necessary to be an active and responsive participant in the birth experience. (In order to birth, the musculature of the legs, back, abdomen, and pelvic floor must release to allow the uterus to labour with no resistance).

- Provides a pregnant woman with the experience and model of loving, nurturing touch that encourages her to touch her baby lovingly.

Relaxation

Relaxation is the key to a calm, comfortable pregnancy. Whether it is through massage, hypnosis, aromatherapy, a warm bath or some other activity, which you find calming and enjoyable. Relaxation encourages your body to release endorphins, your own natural feel good drug. These hormones flow through your body when you relax, laugh, during sex and massage and contribute to your overall sense of well-being. The hormones also cross the placenta to your baby providing the same feel good reaction in his/her little body. Relaxation during pregnancy teaches your baby the skills needed to be a calm, happy little person.

Aromatherapy

Aromatherapy is a natural and beautiful way to help induce feelings of calm and confidence as you approach one of the most powerful experiences in your life as a woman.

Oils can be used in a variety of ways. In baths, foot and hand treatments, as compresses, for inhalation and in self and/or partner massage to help ease tension, restore vitality and alleviate minor ailments of pregnancy.

Conditions that respond well to aromatherapy include respiratory difficulties, high blood pressure, insomnia, nausea, stretch marks, fluid retention, cystitis, vaginal infections and varicose veins.

A growing body of research provides evidence for the benefits of using aromatherapy as a gentle, safe and natural way to nourish the skin, calm the mind and relieve troublesome minor ailments.

The essence of the oils is transported through your breath or skin into your bloodstream. Some oils work directly on the circulation, others travel on to other tissue and organs in your body. Some regulate metabolism, while others act as neuro-chemicals, effecting your emotion.

Essential oils have a remarkable effect on both the body and the mind. They can help alleviate tension and depression. Restore energy, improve sleep, and fight off bacteria. Stimulate cell production, aid digestion, improve circulation of your blood and lymphatic systems and stimulate sexual response.

There are hundreds of essential oils to choose from. However, **because they are very concentrated, during pregnancy it's best to use just a small number that have been tried and tested for their gentle action and safety during pregnancy.** There are some essential oils that should be avoided during pregnancy. The following oils are suitable for use during pregnancy: lavender; rose; chamomile; jasmine (only after 37 weeks); rose geranium; ylang ylang; bergamot; lemon, mandarin, neroli; tangerine; and peppermint.

Aromatherapy offers a stimulating and strengthening energy to draw on during this special time. Your goal is a positive balance and a harmony of mind, body and spirit. Develop your inner strength and accept empowerment.

Blends to try (please check with a qualified aromatherapist for the correct clinical use of essential oils.

- **Relaxing and Refreshing** – lavender and bergamot (bath).
- **Sleep inducing, Sedative** – chamomile on its own or ylang ylang and bergamot (bath or 4 drops on scarf under pillow).
- **Strengthening and Stimulating** – lavender and mandarin (spritz).
- **Decongestant** – lemon and lavender (vapour/inhale).
- **Aphrodisiac** (endorphin release) – ylang ylang and sandalwood (bath, massage, vapour).
- **Anti-stretch mark** – lavender and neroli (massage with avocado or jojoba oil).
- **Cooling** – peppermint (blend with milk or carrier oil for bath).
- **To Relieve Aches and Pains** – chamomile and lavender (massage).

References

Australia's Welfare (2003). AIHW. AIHW Cat. No. AUS 41. Canberra: AIHW.

Benson, H. (1996). *Timeless Healing: The Power and Biology of Belief.* Stark Books, USA.

Buckley, S. (2002). Ecstatic birth - nature's hormonal blueprint for labor. *Mothering Magazine,* issue 111, March-April 2002

Chamberlain, D. (2003).
Prenatal, Birth and New Born Trauma And The Development of a H ealthy Sense of Self.
www.mindenergybodyinstitute.com/PDFs/prenatal.pdf

Dick-Read, Grantly (2004), *Childbirth without Fear: The Principles and Practice of Natural Childbirth.* Pinter & Martin: London.

Dillbeck, M.C., Orme-Johnson, D. (1987). Use of transcendental mediation to relieve stress and promote health. *British Journal of Nursing,* Vol. 4(6), pp 315 – 318.

Fawcett, M. (1988). *Aromatherapy for Pregnancy and Childbirth.* Healing Arts Press. England.

Haley, J. (1986). *Uncommon Therapy: The Psychiatric Techniques of Milton Erickson MD.* W. W. Norton and Company: New York.

Kerry Tuschhoff, (2003) *What is hypnosis for birth and does it work?*
www.hypnobabies.org

Mehl LE. (1994). Hypnosis and conversion of the breech to the vertex presentation. *Archives of Family Medicine, 3(10),* pp 881-887.

Melzack, R., & Wall, P.D. (1965). Pain mechanisms: A new theory. *Science, 150,* pp 171-179.

Odent, M. (1999). Is the Participation of the Father at Birth Dangerous? *Midwifery Today,* Issue 51.

Pert, C. (1999). *Molecules Of Emotion: The Science Between Mind-Body Medicine.* Scribner; USA.

Pratt, G., Wood., & Alman, B. (1988). *A Clinical Hypnosis Primer.* John Wiley and Sons, Inc.; Canada.

Streeter, M. (2004). *Hypnosis: Unlock the Power of Your Mind.* ABC Books, Sydney.